The Pacem Papers

essays on the intersection of
religion, politics, technology,
culture and international relations

Dan Jahn

raven publications

an imprint of The Raven Group

The Pacem Papers
essays on the intersection of religion, politics,
technology, culture and international relations

Copyright © 2011 by Dan Jahn.

Raven Publications | ravenpublications.com
209 Kalamath Street Unit One Denver Colorado 80223-1343

First eBook Edition: April 2011
First US Print Edition: April 2011

Raven Publications is a trademark of The Raven Group, LLC.

ISBN: 978-0-9833211-3-2
eISBN: 978-0-9833211-4-9

10 9 8 7 6 5 4 3 2 1

Dedication

This collection of essays is dedicated to my mom, who "got" to read them all. And to Larry, who didn't.

Acknowledgements

Thanks to my eagle-eyed editor Madigan Talmage-Bowers, who brought my British and American punctuation mashups into sync.

Preface

I believe that the communications technology now being implemented and under continuing rapid development may create a society in a global sense, but one structured around individuals and smaller communities participating in a world-society through technology. Such a scenario may result in a global two-class system: information-rich and information-poor, which could obliterate national boundaries, perhaps wiping out the viability of the concept of the modern nation-state.

If this is the case, I wonder how nationalism and religion will be affected? How would war be waged in such a world, and on what grounds would differences be resolved? This leads to discussion on technology-based and -influenced ethics, and the process of conflict resolution across many boundaries. In that ever-shrinking world—where people are brought into conflict across cultural, ethnic, religious and national boundaries—emerging technology could serve as a medium for conflict resolution.

It is difficult to predict how religions will respond to these worldwide changes, but it seems that there is an argument to be made that there will be a recreation of local communities in a global society —"Gemeinschaft" and "Gesellschaft." Religion needs to—and will do —more than simply respond to these changes; in fact, an inherently peaceful global society cannot become a reality unless disparate religious belief systems are accounted for. Thus I seek to understand the dynamics of the interplay between religion, technology and politics/international relations.

I make a basic assumption that "knowledge = improved relations," i.e., the more conflicting parties know about one another's underlying precepts, the better the chance for resolution, and the creation of a just, peaceful and sustainable global society which maintains cultural uniqueness.

Dan Jahn
January 2011
Denver, CO

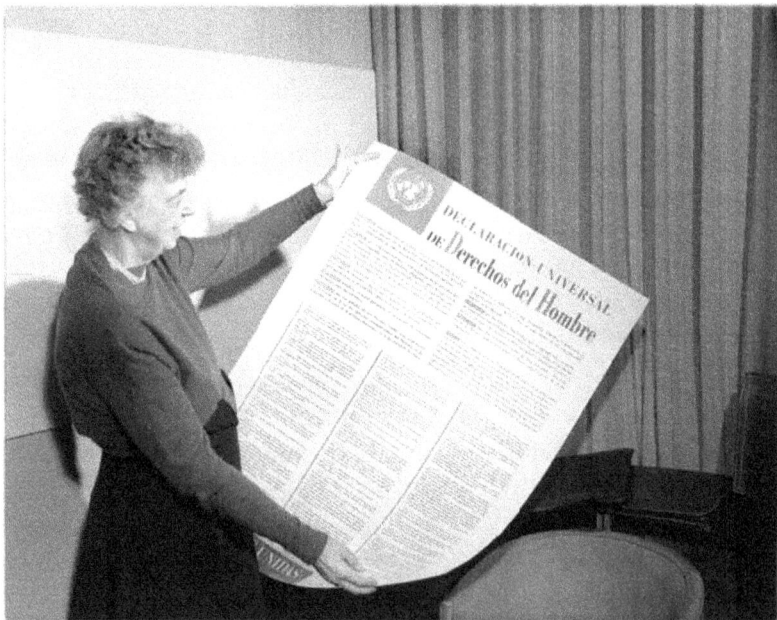

DECLARACION UNIVERSAL DE Derechos del Hombre

UN PHOTO

Comparing Conceptions of Human Rights

Towards an Understanding of

Human Rights in Islam

INTRODUCTION

The world, through the nation-state paradigm, has reached consensus on many issues, but a significant number remain points of contention. In those continuing debates, human rights sits as a reigning champion of disunity. Secular notions of human rights are themselves in disagreement on many philosophical points, and are to varying degrees in contention with one another and with Christian conceptualizations of human rights. In the global context—on a variety of "sub-issues" such as abortion, women's rights, etc.—the clash between East and West on human rights is often characterized as the enlightened West struggling against the ignorance and stubbornness of Islam. This paper serves as an inquiry into that particular (Middle) East vs. West debate, striving to understand Islamic notions of human rights in relation to Christian, Marxist, Classical and post-modern secular ideas of human rights.

Human rights as an idea—although certainly a contemporary debate in the West—is central to the historical socio-political development of the West, and finds its roots as a philosophical debate in the medieval European discussions on morality. Human rights as it is currently debated is fundamentally a Western idea; a significant reason for its lack of progress is its historical rejection of non-Western conceptions—grounded perhaps most solidly in the philosophical writings of 17th century Englishman John Locke.

The idea of human rights arising out of Locke's social contract theories have been subsequently challenged and expanded by Western philosophers, theologians and politicians, and have been codified in documents such as the *United States Declaration of Independence* (1776), the *United States Bill of Rights* (1789), the *French Declaration of the Rights of Man* (1789), and the *United Nations Declaration of Human Rights* (1948). All of these documents are attempts to put into writing "universal laws" which pertain to the rights of humans. But the question begged by these documents is the origin of the rights proclaimed therein —and the relevance of that claim of origin to disparate religious traditions—and it is here that the clash with Islam begins.

To reach a point of understanding in a discussion of human rights debates in modern times, a brief overview of human rights in the West must be undertaken, and then viewed in relation to Islamic notions of humanity and its rights, with the understanding that the basic Western point of view is prevalent, and is inescapable in the contemporary debate.

The West long ago agreed on the "preferability of life in a society with human rights," because in such a society "you would never be without the status and protection of those rights."[1] In order to achieve such a society, the society as a whole must agree on exactly what rights humans have simply by virtue of being human. Ethical theories are thus constructed to supply the basis for these rights. The basis of these theories was Christianity and Christianity-derived ethics, and remains so for many today. Moral philosophers since the 18th century have tried to remove the Christian element from the theories to put forth secular notions of human rights on the grounds that such formulations are inherently more universal, but here we have our first problem, which is "To whom are these more acceptable in their universality?" Even Christians, although they may accept that the rights as they are written are universal, will still disagree with the basis for them, and Muslims for the most part will simply reject them in toto for not having been framed in Islamic terms, by Islamic theologians, or more correctly, Islamic legal theorists.

Thus we in the West are confronted with the necessity of performing an act of bricolage, of bringing together our own Western philosophical perspectives—with our secular yet Christian derived traditions of human rights—with the perspective on Islam gained through religious studies. Obviously, our concern is not with the historical record of how adherents of various traditions have acted with regard to their beliefs on human rights, but with the traditions themselves; in trying to frame a human rights dialogue among religions and socio-cultural traditions, the concern is with the constantly developing framework given to believers to shape their actions, and the resulting multi-national agreements based on those frameworks which arise in modernity. To further the discussion and strive for global agreement on human rights, we must determine what an acceptable theory of rights should contain, formulate that theory, and then attempt to justify the elements of the theory within various ideologies, including secular, Christian, Muslim, and even Marxist. This is obviously a nigh-impossible task, but we can at least postulate what (from a Western perspective) these ethical theories of human rights must contain.

THE ELEMENTS OF HUMAN RIGHTS

Hugo Bedau has put forth a useful summary of the elements a theory of human rights must contain at an absolute minimum. Bedau states that no current theory of human rights can meet the criteria he lays down[2], but in a sense this is wrong. By making that judgment on current human rights theories, Bedau shows his bias in relation to religious concepts of the rights of man. The essence of a religious doctrine of human rights is that it is inherently universal by virtue of its basis in God, and thus automatically meets these criteria. The problem for the religious human rights activist in any tradition is convincing the rest of humanity of the universality of the religion itself, be it Christianity or Islam or other. Bedau is certainly correct in his assessment of the current theories within the secular context, but doesn't admit to that context within his essay. It is along these same lines that such documents as the *United Nations Declaration* fails, and the *United States Bill of Rights* is also beginning to fail. They are incapable of addressing the belief systems of an increasingly diverse population, all clamoring for "equal rights," both human and otherwise.

We must also realize that the issue of human rights has come to the forefront of the international scene after the revelation of the shocking abuse of human rights epitomized by the acts of genocide carried out primarily against the Jewish population of Europe by the Nazis—which puts the issue into a religious context for at least one group of people from the outset—and also from the abuse of its citizens by the former Soviet Union that are still being revealed. Thus the contemporary West is responding to a Western event, and is of course framing a Western response. The difficulty in then applying that response globally is obvious, so some other course must be taken.

We can however-drawing on Hugo Bedau's work—look at any theory of human rights and ask of it the following questions:

a) What is its concept of human rights? This presupposes that the theory has an understanding of the uniqueness of human rights, distinct from other kinds of rights;

b) Can it provide a fairly conclusive list of specific human rights or a set method for determining the validity of a claim to a right specified as human? This is essential to eventual codification of these rights worldwide;

c) What are the categories into which human rights can be sorted? This is absolutely necessary in addressing changing situations;

d) What is the understanding of the origin of human rights? This question is crucial in the context of religion and politics, (somewhat ignored by Bedau, even though he posits the necessity of its inclusion in a general theory);

e) What is the role played by human rights within the framework of an overarching moral theory? Again, a question that must be answered for varying religious traditions;

f) Can it give an accounting of the priorities of human rights? For instance, in situations where violation of one person's or one group's rights affect the rights of another, as in hostage situations; and finally,

g) How does the theory address the enforceability of these rights? This presupposes an agreement of institutions capable of enforcing them, and agreement on the method of enforcement.[3]

THE SOURCES OF WESTERN HUMAN RIGHTS

We can ask these questions of the major Western traditions, based on J. Bryan Hehir's assessment of the four main sources of human rights claims in the West: the Classical, formulated by Cicero; the Christian idea, as put forth by Pope John XXIII; the Liberal or Lockean idea of human rights, based on John Locke's philosophy; and the Marxist conception, (e.g., Marx)[4], and ask these same questions of Islam in comparative perspective in order to reach a more conclusive point for dialogue with Islam on human rights issues. We in the West often assume that each of these ideologies has a conception of human rights. This, in fact, is a bit disingenuous, as of course in all traditions people have asked the question, "What is my or my community's concept of human rights?" Having posed the question, they have sought to justify a position taken by themselves as normative by drawing analogies within their respective traditions to their ideas of a human right. We are not concerned here, however, with posing each of these questions, but only with those that lead to an understanding of ethical frameworks, and thus possibly to what Henry Rosemont has called similarities in "concept clusters",[5] namely, the question dealing with the concept of human rights in disparate traditions. Obviously, this involves some de-contextualizing of these concepts, with the attempt to re-contextualize them in modernity and globalization, rather than limiting them to only their respective cultural milieus.

For both Classical theorists and Christians, human rights presupposes a recognition of the intrinsic worth of the human being, and views the dignity of the human as the over-riding concern in matters of rights. In the debate between Classical and Christian rights theorists, the basic assumption is that natural law is the governing ideology, and rights can be extracted from that position. As Hehir points out, however, the question of transcendence divides the two camps rather decisively, and it is here the conception of human rights in the two sources begins to be delineated, where Classical rights exist for a human being in a closed universe, and rights for humans from a Christian perspective are rooted in a transcendent source.[6] Richard Harries puts human rights in theological perspective for Christians by taking as a beginning point that "rights are grounded...in the value of the created order,"[7] and furthermore those rights are recognized by God himself, in that he has created man in his own image and therefore "respects the worth and dignity of what he has created."[8] It is this perspective on human rights which Pope John XXIII put forth in *Pacem in Terris*, where human rights is placed within the framework of redemption and grace[9] while simultaneously allowing that philosophical inquiry into the actualization of human rights is both acceptable and desirable.

Here we have a key distinction in process from Islam: whereas Christian sources for inquiry and comment on human matters since World War II have been institutional—in the form of the Vatican and the World Council of Churches[10]—Islam is not constructed around a central authority, and thus has no similar mechanism for pronouncement on such issues. Prior to the events of World War II and historically, individual theologians played a much larger role in Christian theology, much as individual scholars (*ulama*) and jurists (*fuquha*) practiced *ijtihad* (the *Qur'an*- and Hadith-sanctioned method of reaching decisions through independent reasoning) to formulate Islamic responses to changing times. The gates of *ijtihad* were closed under the Abbasid Dynasty, thus adding to the difficulty of formulating an Islamic conception of human rights.

Islam does agree with Christianity in one essential fact, in that Islam also holds mankind to be unique and worthy of dignity, with that dignity affirmed by Allah: "We have called noble (*karramuna*) the sons of Adam."[11] But Islam does not grant man rights simply by that uniqueness, as does Christian and Jewish theology. All rights of man in Islam derive only as a version of claim-rights, in that Allah has promised certain things to those who totally submit to his will (who become a Muslim). In fact, in its references to the duties (*farud*) of men, Islam is more in line with Hindu notions of *dharma* than it is with Christian ideas of human rights. The Hindu sees himself as having been born into a specific set of circumstances, with a set of duties which must be performed in order to progress spiritually. Obviously, Islam differs here with Hinduism in that the same duties are given to all men, regardless of the circumstances of their birth, and there perhaps lies some hope for a specifically Islamic human rights ethic.

John Locke also took issue with part of the Christian framework, and while agreeing with natural law doctrine, questioned the social position of man. The Christian point of view states that man is inherently social, and therefore the development of humanity only takes place within a community. In Locke's social contract idea, human beings are intrinsically self-sufficient, and thus join a community only because life is easier in a community setting.[12] Here we see similarities between Christianity and Islam, in that the essential ingredient of an Islamic worldview is the establishment of the *umma*, the worldwide community of Muslims. Questions as to whether this community is more spiritual in nature (and thus each person who converts to Islam is entering the *umma*), or whether the realization of the *umma* does in fact require complete conversion to Islam on the part of all humans is a point of dissension within Islam itself, but need not be solved in order for human rights to be addressed. Here Locke's social contract ideas are useful, as they can be seen to be reflected in Islam to some extent, in the strict obligations of each member of the community to act in a certain way which helps to preserve the community. The centrality of *communitas* to both Christianity and Islam may also provide a starting point for dialogue on the rights of humans within those communities, although how rights are addressed for members of Christian (or Jewish or Buddhist, for that matter) communities who find themselves within an Islamic community, or vice-versa, is an issue of great concern in the modern context. Islam itself has provided for such situations in its concept of *dhimmi*, whereby religious minority members of the community pay a tax (*jizya*) to avoid duties incumbent on Muslim members of the community, but this itself is contrary to Western ideals of human rights. Scholars such as James Piscatori, Majid Khadduri and others have concluded that non-Muslims (*dhimmis*) are second-class citizens under such a system, citing the various restrictions placed upon them by the Islamic government.

Again, preservation of the greater community—the physical community of an ever-shrinking world—can perhaps provide the basis for dialogue between the two traditions. Obviously, the problem is that the assertion of individual rights eventually runs counter to the needs of the community. Philosophers have been agonizing over solving this problem, and politicians have proposed list after list of rights, but the problem is that no agreement on process has yet been reached. Agreement on concept clusters and agreement on a process can at least provide some hope of dialogue on this issue, but final resolution is simply not attainable in the context of universal legislation such as the *United Nations Declaration*.

Marxist doctrine offers an interesting perspective on the concept of human rights when discussing it in the context of communities. The Marxist tradition comes from the standpoint of challenging the Liberal Case for endowing humans with certain inalienable rights which protect them from the possibility of abuse by the state.[13] Marxist human rights are instead claim-rights, in the sense that they are rights which a person may demand that the state provides, thus protecting the state's status as the best of all possible structures, in that the state provides assurance that each person lives "decently." The danger in the Marxist doctrine is obviously that it can lead to communism and totalitarianism, but it can also lead to liberation theology, as Gustavo Gutiérrez has eloquently formulated in his essays. But Marxism has deeper problems; as Wesley Hohfield[14] has pointed out, claim-rights have correlating duties, and as we have seen, the concept of duties plays an important role in Islam. Marxism fails to provide an adequate framework for human rights because it fails to clearly outline these duties, leaving a vacuum in the fabric of morality. Marxist doctrine also seems to claim that there are no other types of rights, a rather unlikely basis for constructing a successful human rights framework for multiple cultures.

In attempting to lay down international rules by which nations must abide regarding human rights or face consequences, we in the West are forcing some Muslims to cite the *Qur'an* as a source for moral statements on human rights. Although there are examples in the Muslim holy text of direct concern with rights—for example, the verses dealing with the place of women, and those condemning the practice of infanticide—for the most part, Muslims are responding to the West through acontextual exegesis. Islamic rights activists are attributing human rights morality theories to the *Qur'an* without really considering the ways by which the meaning of its moral concepts were developed in the context of the sixth century Arabian peninsula. The simple fact is that Islam's development of a combined spiritual and temporal government does not lead to a concept of individual human rights in relation to the state, either in Marxist dependency terms or in Lockean social contract terms, and any attempt to legislate across national boundaries will therefore be doomed to failure.

We in the West are moving ahead on human rights laws for the international community without attempting to understand the cultures upon which we are trying place behavioral restrictions. An attempt must be made to interpret the moral vocabulary of Islam before Western philosophers continue to put forth theories. Obviously, that attempt should involve what this essay involved, that is, a comparison to our own Western traditions. Once that has been done, however, perhaps Western, Muslim and Eastern scholars as well can agree on a process by which to continue the dialogue, given an awareness of their biases, and perhaps formulate a new way of framing ethical attitudes with an expanded global awareness. There is not a tradition of human rights per se in Islam, any more than there is in Christian or Western viewpoints. However, there is a tradition of developing moral attitudes, which can find agreement on process and on the necessity of protecting people from evil. Whether that process can result in a meaningful international declaration remains to be seen, but it is doubtful that such a declaration would succeed in a world of nation-states and sovereignty issues.

SUGGESTIONS FOR FURTHER READING

Ally, Muhammed Mashuq Ibn, "Theology of Islamic Liberation," in *World Religions and Human Liberation*, ed. Dan Cohn-Sherbock. Maryknoll, New York: Orbis Books, 1992.

Becker, Lawrence C. "Individual Rights," in *And Justice for All*, eds. Tom Regan and Donald VanDeVeer. Totawa, New Jersey: Rowman and Littlefield, 1982.

Bedau, Hugo Adam, "International Human Rights," in *And Justice for All*, eds. Tom Regan and Donald VanDeVeer. Totowa, New Jersey: Rowman and Littlefield, 1982.

Gutiérrez, Gustavo. "Option for the poor: review and challenges," in *The Month*, January 1995, 5-10.

Harries, Richard. "Human rights in theological perspective," in *Human Rights for the 1990s: Legal, Political and Ethical Issues*, eds. Robert Blackburn and John Taylor. London: Mansell Publishing Limited, 1991, 1-13.

Hehir, J. Bryan. "Human Rights From a Theological Perspective," in *The Moral Imperatives of Human Rights: A World Survey*, ed. Kenneth W. Thompson. Washington, DC: University Press of America, 1980, 1-21.

Hawwa, Saeed. *The Muslim Brotherhood*, Abdul Karim Shaikh, trans. Kuwait: Al faisal Islamic Press, 1985.

Heper, Martin, and Raphael Israeli, eds. *Islam and Politics in the Modern Middle East*. London: Croom Helm, 1984.

Mayer, Ann. *Islam and Human Rights: Traditions and Politics*. Boulder, CO: Westview Press, 1991.

Piscatori, James. "Human Rights in Islamic Political Culture," in *The Moral Imperatives of Human Rights: A World Survey*, ed. Kenneth W. Thompson. Washington, DC: University Press of America, 1980, 139-167.

Rouner, Leroy S. ed. *Human Rights and the World's Religions*. Notre Dame: University of Notre Dame Press, 1988.

Inquiry Into A Western Fear

Islamic Social Justice

INTRODUCTION

If one can point to an overarching characteristic of our time, concern with justice would surely be near the top of the list. Never in the history of man has there been such a quest for justice, a quest pursued by both individuals and groups in all walks of life and around the world. In this quest, religions have played a vital role, while at the same time, religious movements are continually misunderstood and mis-characterized by opposing groups. The Muslim movements which the Western media refer to as representative of a dangerous Islamic fundamentalism with militant overtones is one example where a misunderstanding has resulted in widespread fear and prohibited what could potentially be a useful partnership. It is not an exaggeration to say that upon hearing the words "Muslim Brotherhood," many otherwise educated Westerners tend to think only of a terrorist organization, and it is not inconceivable to think that some Muslims may in fact look at the World Council of Churches as yet another example of Western imperialism. The truth is that although Islamic fundamentalism or perhaps more appropriately "revivalism" does have its extremists, a major focal point of some Muslim movements is an attempt to balance the scales of social justice in much the same way that the Christians of the West—through the World Council of Churches—are attempting to rectify situations of poverty, abuse of human rights and other social issues. This is not to dismiss the violence inherent in some Islamic fundamentalist movements, merely to show that the terrorist-like activities of these movements are emphatically not the movements' main program of action, and are, for instance in the case of the Muslim Brotherhood, more a reaction to events of the time that many organizations, including the Brotherhood, responded to in a violent manner.

KINDS OF JUSTICE

There are various kinds of justice, and emphasis on certain kinds of justice varies from society to society. One kind of justice can be called positive justice, and is part of a worldview that centers around rational man; an assumption that men are capable of determining their individual or collective interests and can therefore establish rules by which justice is to be served. As social change occurs, the rules are re-evaluated and adjusted accordingly. A second kind of justice assumes that men are incapable of rising above personal failings and therefore justice relies on revelation sources. This can be called Divine justice, and is the basis for the ancient Hebrew, Christian and Islamic worldview, in which the concept of justice is related to the interaction between God's will and mankind's destiny, although elements of positive justice finally enter into all three traditions at various times. In all of these religious traditions, there is and always has been a preeminent concern with justice. In Christianity, this synthesis of Divine and positive justice is called the Eternal Law by St. Thomas Aquinas in his *Summa Theologica* and is called *shar'ia* by Muslims.

This justice can be discussed in terms of several more specific areas, including theology, ethics, and legalities, but what is of increasing current concern is the way in which these religious traditions deal with questions of social justice. The topic most often spoken of is human rights, an issue of major importance in international relations as states fight for sovereignty within their borders, yet also fight to be recognized as equals at the bargaining tables of international diplomacy—not the least of which are the various councils of the United Nations. An understanding of how religions succeed in dispensing social justice is crucial to developing an understanding of how these religions are affecting political processes in the international arena. This essay therefore provides a brief study of Islamic social justice ideas, by first giving a brief introduction to the theological source for social justice, providing some historical background on several prominent Islamic movements concerned with social issues and pointing to some specific actions, and in conclusion, addressing what might be called the relative religious success of Muslim social action.

SOCIAL JUSTICE IN ISLAM

The theological basis for social justice in Islam differs from Christianity in one important sense, in that concern with social issues is an essential part of the ritualization of Islam, through the "Pillars of the Faith" laid down by Muhammed. The Five Pillars constitute a set of rules which must be obeyed by every Muslim—for Islam is a remarkably coherent religion, despite its various permutations—to the best of his ability, in order for that person to claim with any truth that he is in fact a Muslim (one who submits to God). One such "rule" is the second pillar, which involves the payment of *zakat*, a percentage of annual revenue which is to be used for the benefit of the poor and various works of charity. This money is usually given to a local authority, who then distributes the money according to its various programs. One area in which there is some disparity in Islam is in what varying Muslims recognize as the local authorities, which can take the form of certain social movements, or mosques; the money is also given directly to the poor in some areas. Inasmuch as Christianity came out of Judaism, so in many respects did Islam, and there is overwhelming evidence for the Judaic character of this term (*zakat*), in which the acquiring of merit for oneself is indissoluble from the act of giving away a proportion of one's wealth for the poor. Islam disapproves of people in need...and *zakat* provides the state with adequate means of maintaining the welfare of all in the community (*umma*).

To speak of theological justifications for something in Islam is in itself misleading, as theology was never the pre-eminent force that it has been in Christianity until very recently. Islamic lawyers have historically had much more importance than Islamic theologians in virtually every Muslim community, including the two main divisions of Islam, the Sunni and the

Shii. The Shii are the main minority (constituting about 15% of the world's population of Muslims, as opposed to 85% Sunni), and among other differences, can be characterized by a messianic appeal to an ideal of justice, and a rejection of the established authorities. The Shii still, even with their hostility to authorities, do not spend much time in theological reflection. Rather than looking purely to lawyers as do the Sunni, the Shii also look to infallible *imams*, or religious leaders. The Sunni have no infallible leaders calling upon them to perform certain actions, but in their communities also is the absolute rule of *zakat*, and across the Islamic world concern for the needy is of tantamount importance.

We can look to Muhammed for the initial concern with social issues, as Muhammed was in essence a reformer, certainly in terms of religious ideals. In fact, he could be called a social reformer. He instituted legislation that improved the status of women, pushed for the emancipation of slaves, and prohibited things that he saw as unjust and immoral, including infanticide. Here we see the beginnings of the Islamic concern with human rights, which are also borne out in the holy text of Islam, the *Qur'an*. The *Qur'an* is liberally sprinkled with various references to justice, including this one, perhaps the most important Qur'anic references to justice:

> God commands justice and good-doing....
> (Q. XV, 92)

> ...and when you judge among men, you
> should judge with justice. (Q. IV, 61)7

We see a real attempt in Islam to practically apply the concept of social justice in the work of Muslim thinkers such as Ibn Taymiya and Najm al-Din al-Tawfi, who both talked about the benefits of social justice to all Islam, in the spiritual *jihad* for the hearts and souls of the world. "Social justice," Taymiya argued, would "ultimately improve social conditions" and thus "enhance the power of Islam." Taymiya lived in the late 1200s, in what he perceived as a time of decadence, and thus much of his concern with social justice was on the level of returning Islam to its former powerful status. His writings were preceded by several others, but Taymiya's writings, along with contemporary Najm al-Tawfi's, are really the predecessor to modern Islamic concerns with social justice. Najm al-Din al-Tawfi put public interest ahead of all other sources for law—a form of positive justice—which tended to promote the general welfare of the Muslim people. Several writers continued to follow this tradition, and in modern times, the Islamic conception of justice has continued along these lines, metamorphosing from the early abstract idea of Divine justice to an idea of social justice as being central to Islamic theology, and more importantly, to the daily life of Muslims around the world. Partially as a result of increased contact with Western values and legal systems, Muslims have become more aware of their laws, and in consequence, have set social justice concepts at the apex of their interactions. This is again a reflection of spiritual *jihad*, but here the battle is for the hearts and souls of fellow Muslims.

MUSLIM GROUPS

More and more concerned with the plight of other Muslims, the Islamic world-wide community looks to ideas of social justice to bolster the status of Islam. In response to public concern about Islam's status in the lives of Muslims battered by modernity, several Muslim groups were formed to specifically address questions of social justice, the most prominent of which are the Muslim Brotherhood (Ikhwan al-Muslimoon) in Egypt, and the Islamic Society (Jamaat-i-Islami) in Pakistan. There are many other Islamic movements, some more militant than others. These two organizations are important because they were both founded largely in response to the West, and are thus looked at as anti-Western and therefore dangerous, and also because they have both become very widespread. They are both primarily concerned with a form of gradual adaptation, rather than revolutionary tactics, such as the Islamic revival groups al-Jihad (Egypt), Hizbullah (Lebanon), and the Islamic Republican Party (Iran). Although the reputation of the Muslim Brotherhood for political violence is not without justification, it is not the primary motive of the society.

One aspect of the success of a movement is simply how widespread the movement becomes, and in both the Muslim Brotherhood and in Jamaat-i-Islami we have organizations which have world-wide appeal for Muslims. The Brotherhood has inspired movements with similar aims and goals in the Sudan, Syria, Jordan, the Gulf and Africa; the Jamaat-i-Islami now has affiliated organizations in India, Bangladesh, Afghanistan and Kashmir. Both organizations have sympathizers in many countries, not the least of which are the United States, Saudi Arabia, and Great Britain.

In both of these movements, one can sense not an ingrained hostility towards the West per se, but certainly a feeling of being entrapped by encircling Western cultural values, secular nationalism, and Western imperialism. Often ignored by popular media personalities reporting on Islam is the fact that these movements have similar feelings—a general rejection—towards the irreligious values of Marxism and its materialist tendencies. The point of both of these organizations is to point out to Muslims feeling overwhelmed by Marxist or Western values that neither alternative is viable, and that Islam is in itself a complete answer to the challenges of modernity. Each movement is an attempt to come to terms with the realities of modern life and modify Islamic standards in order to fit Muslim societies into an increasingly globally interdependent world, but they differ in what core beliefs constitute an adherence to Islam while still insuring social justice and a place in the circle of modern nation-states.

THE MUSLIM BROTHERHOOD

The Muslim Brotherhood was founded in 1928 by Hasan al-Banna, but did not achieve real prominence until shortly after World War II. The Brotherhood began to reproach young men who were attracted to foreign economic systems, and told them that Islam was in fact ideally formulated for economic survival in modern times. Islam, the Brotherhood asserted, recognizes private ownership and indeed "the right of disposition and the transfer of property," provided that public interest and the general welfare of the Muslim community takes precedence. Islam also urges believers to exploit natural resources, as long as the good of the general Muslim community is of tantamount importance in such dealings. Central to the belief structure of the Muslim Brotherhood is the concept of "just standards" upon which society must be based. As long as this concept is underlying any change, industrialization and related activities of modernization can be accommodated. A belief in free enterprise with a large role for the state in economics is a core belief; the Brotherhood further states that all public utilities should be nationalized, and various other measures should be taken in order to ensure a balance between freedom and equality, with equality being the pinnacle of social justice. The understanding of equality being literally equated with justice is a key difference between the Muslim Brotherhood and the Jamaat-i-Islami.

JAMAAT-I-ISLAMI

The Jamaat-i-Islami was founded in Pakistan in 1941 by Abul Ala Mawdudi, and similar to the Muslim Brotherhood, finds the majority of its most stringent adherents in the educated young men of the middle class. The movement advocates the "Islamisation" of politics and society, stating that religion and politics are indivisible. Economically, these Muslims stress individual ownership more than the Brotherhood, and reject state ownership, particularly of land. The movement's concern with social justice is not merely with distributive justice, as is the Brotherhood's. The assertion here is that Islam is by nature just, and the establishment of a truly Islamic state serves the purpose of social justice. Thus the Jamaat-i-Islami strove to create in Pakistan an Islamic republic, but were defeated in this by the framers of the constitutions of Pakistan. They are still concerned with the ideal of an Islamic nation-state, and look to Iran for inspiration.

Both organizations are involved on a daily basis with combating social inequality on a massive scale. Despite the Western media's claims, not all Muslim movements are oriented towards terrorist activities, and a brief examination of the activities of these two groups certainly bears this out. Before discussing specific activities, an area of general concern should be mentioned. One issue of social concern in the West has been racism, particularly the case of South African apartheid, which has of course recently changed for the better. It is worth pointing out—since racism is of such concern in the West—that Islam itself is against racism (although individuals still harbor personal prejudices), and thus has no "Programs to Combat Racism," as does the World Council of Churches. Islam sought to accord the individual a higher level of esteem and self-respect, recognizing no distinction among believers–such as race, class or color–save their membership in Islam (Q. XLIX, 10).

WOMEN'S RIGHTS

An additional area of concern in Western minds is women's rights. Here again, Islam and members of the Brotherhood and the Jamaat-i-Islami are actually far more progressive than many people are willing to admit. In the eyes of Islam, women are the equals of men. Islam resisted the early tribal notion that a girl child was a disaster, and raised her status. What must be understood is that Muhammed, while indeed a social reformer, had to work within the limits of his time, and accomplished quite a bit towards elevating women, although he was too wise a man to go to extremes at the time. In modern Islam, even the spokesman and general guide of the Brotherhood (Hasan al-Hudaybi) admitted that women can pursue almost anything a man can, and of his own daughters he took pride in the fact that the elder is now a doctor and practices professionally. The second is a graduate of the Faculty of Science and is now a teacher.

These religious organizations must be more than ideologically progressive, however, and must be benefiting their fellow man at some level; they must be succeeding to some extent, or the movements would have long ago died out. The Muslim Brotherhood would have ended with its suppression by Gamal Abd al-Nasir in the mid-1950s, and the Jamaat-i-Islami would have ended with the creation of Pakistan. But, as we know, both movements have continued and in fact seem to be growing in the midst of what appears to be a worldwide religious revivalism. What maintains the momentum of these movements is their pro-active role in the daily lives of Muslims around the world.

In the 1980s, the Muslim Brotherhood was very active at a grass-roots level, as mainstream-based popular support for the Brotherhood and its activities began to emerge, and the organization built and supported Islamic medical clinics and various social welfare organizations. Even prior to the 1980s, the

Brotherhood was involved in studying farm exploitation and labor organizations with an eye towards correcting abuses, helping students make a more profitable use of their studies, and forming a variety of small committees to help people in all walks of life deal with day-to-day concerns. The Jamaat-Islami is also involved with educational programs, medical centers and general assistance to Muslims in need in almost every area in which the movement is based.

The two largest religions in the world, Christianity and Islam, have specific ways of dealing with social issues, and these ways meet with varying success in purely physical terms. More importantly, they also meet with varying religious success. In order to survive, all religions must appear to be continuing to successfully assist humankind in its disparate crises. In the case of Islam, the religion is fighting battles on several fronts; the leaders of the fundamentalist groups see the temptations of the West diverting some Muslims from Islam, but they are also confronted with the basic questions of social justice we have outlined here. In fighting this multi-faceted battle, some Muslims have come to the conclusion that the battle against the West should in fact become more pronounced, and thus engage in terrorist activities. This is emphatically not the same battle that is being fought by many Muslims against social inequalities and the two should not be lumped together, as is the media's wont in the West. This is not to deny the militancy and extremism of the Muslim Brotherhood, but only to say that the whole picture must be shown.

CONCLUSIONS

The success of Islamic social justice is difficult to measure, as is any religious activity, but the actions of the Muslim Brotherhood in helping war-torn families in the aftermath of the Gulf War, and the Jamaat-i-Islami members trying to feed the masses in India, are images that should also be beamed out from CNN's satellites, and not just the terrorist actions of al-Jihad. The Islamic fundamentalist movement is often portrayed as being part of a lower-class, uneducated response to modernity, but in fact the Muslim Brotherhood's membership in the 1990s reflects doctors, engineers, pharmacists, dentists and lawyers, and the movement is achieving renewed success as it dominates professional associations in Egypt and elsewhere.

The Jamaat-i-Islami is also attracting more and more of the emerging middle class of India to its organization, which is furthering its financial status and thus its ability to render assistance. The Islamic world is trying to come to grips with another world, and in the pain of that wrestling match, questions of social justice are being addressed on both sides, in a humane and just manner.

The West must put aside its fears and try to understand both the violence of Islamic revivalism in some cases, and the other side, the social justice side, realizing that there are those Muslims willing to fight the tide of poverty, hunger, and disease that is sweeping both East and West, both North and South.

Ahmad, Mumtaz. *Islamic Fundamentalism in South-Asia: The Jamaat-i-Islami and the Tablighi Jamaat*, in Fundamentalisms Observed,1:457-530, Marty, Martin E. & R. Scott Appleby, eds. Chicago: University of Chicago Press, 1991.

As-Sadr, Muhammed Baqir. *Contemporary Man and The Social Problem*, Yasin T. Al-Jibouri, trans. Iran: World Organization for Islamic Services, 1986.

Baldick, Julian. *Early Islam*, in The Worlds Religions: Islam, ed. Peter Clarke. London: Routledge, 1990, 7-22.

_____. *Islam: The Straight Path*. New York: Oxford University Press, 1991.

Hawwa, Saeed. *The Muslim Brotherhood*, Abdul Karim Shaikh, trans. Kuwait: Al faisal Islamic Press, 1985.

Heper, Martin, and Raphael Israeli, eds. *Islam and Politics in the Modern Middle East*. London: Croom Helm, 1984.

Hunter, Shireen T., ed. *The Politics of Islamic Revivalism*. Bloomington: Indiana University Press, 1988.

Khadduri, Majid. *The Islamic Conception of Justice*. Baltimore: Johns Hopkins University Press, 1984.

Mernissi, Fatima. *Islam and Democracy: Fear of the Modern World*, Mary Jo Lakeland, trans. London: Virago Press, 1993.

Mitchell, Richard P. *The Society of the Muslim Brothers*. New York: Oxford University Press, 1993.

Nash, Manning. *Islamic Resurgence in Malaysia and Indonesia*, in Fundamentalisms Observed,1:691-739, Marty, Martin E. & R. Scott Appleby, eds. Chicago: University of Chicago Press, 1991.

Rouner, Leroy S., ed. *Human Rights and the Worlds Religions*. Notre Dame: University of Notre Dame Press, 1988.

Sachedina, Abdulaziz A. *Activist Shi'ism in Iran, Iraq, and Lebanon*, in Fundamentalisms Observed,1:403-456, Marty, Martin E. & R. Scott Appleby, eds. Chicago: University of Chicago Press, 1991.

Voll, Jon O. *Fundamentalism in the Sunni Arab World: Egypt and the Sudan*, in Fundamentalisms Observed,1:345-402, Marty, Martin E. & R. Scott Appleby, eds. Chicago: University of Chicago Press, 1991.

© Yan Boechat

The Shar'ia

The Backbone

or the Achilles' Heel

of an Islamic State?

INTRODUCTION

As the process of globalization proceeds at an increasingly rapid pace, the Muslim world is being forced to justify itself internally and externally in response to the perceived threat that secularization necessarily follows modernity, and modernity is part and parcel of globalization. Central to this justification is the ongoing debate of the place of Islamic law in a modern nation-state, and the question being asked by Western secularists, Western and Muslim scholars, Muslim conservatives and reformers, politicians, Christians, and Muslim "theologians" is, "What is the role of *shar'ia* within the Islamic state?" That question calls for analysis of the concept and definition of *shar'ia*, how its role has been interpreted historically, how *shar'ia* is being implemented currently, and the relative success of those interpretations. Some conclusions must be drawn on how *shar'ia* can fit into a modern nation-state based on Islamic precepts, such that the state is accepted on equal footing into a world composed of democracies and trans-national, cross-cultural organizations, corporations and governmental alliances.

The literal meaning of *shar'ia* is "the path to the source of water," the implication of which is that it is the source of life for Muslims, and has come to mean the "divinely mandated path"[15] —the clear and correct path that one must follow in life so as to be submitting (as Muslim means literally "one who submits") to the will of God. As such, the *shar'ia* must be central to any Islamic society. *Shar'ia* is what Thomas Aquinas would term "Eternal Law," in that it derives mainly from revelation, and is in fact the embodiment of God's will and justice,[16] though the *shar'ia* is much more than just revelation; it consists of laws drawn from revelation and wisdom, and from consensus and analogy.[17] It is authoritative due to its two textual sources: the *Qur'an*, as God's word revealed to the prophet Muhammad over a period of some years (revelation), and the *sunna* (the trodden path)—the practices and sayings (wisdom) of the prophet Muhammad which became the norm for Muslim behavior and were thus preserved in written form, becoming a collection of traditions (*hadith*) passed down through the centuries since Muhammad's death in June of 632 CE.[18]

VERACITY

The *Qur'an* differs from the *Bible*, in that it is somewhat less disputable, for the entire text was received by one man, over a definite period of time, and thus has perhaps more historical integrity than either the Old or New Testament. The *hadith* do come into question, as the attempt to verify the veracity of claims about the prophet's behavior are difficult to prove, relying as they do on circumstantial evidence and second hand information, but only as regards exactly which of the traditions can definitely be ascribed to Muhammad and which can only "probably" be attributed directly to the prophet. Such critiques of the *hadith* have not been extensive, however, since very early in Islamic history, and therefore what survives today are considered essentially definitive. The *shar'ia* has one additional source, which is derivative rather than absolutely authoritative, and that is due to the Islamic concept of *ijtihad*, human or independent reasoning. The early interpreters of the *shar'ia* after the death of Muhammad relied on the concept of *ijtihad* and sought agreement with one another on decisions and the basis for those decisions (consensus and analogy). Islamic scholars rely on the *shar'ia* to deal with questions about theology, practice, and legal matters, as Islam encompasses both law and religion for Muslims.

JUSTICE

It is important in attempting to determine the role of *shar'ia* to understand that while Islam embodies both law and religion, they are emphatically not the same thing. While both are expressions of God's will and justice, religion defines and determines goals, and law (*shar'ia*) indicates the path by which the goals can be realized. The main goal is essentially justice, as the Muslim understand divine justice to be central to the relationship between man and God and to the relationships between men, and thus the *shar'ia* constitutes the Islamic corpus juris, outlined in its permissions (*halal*), and prohibitions (*haram*).[19] These permissions and prohibitions outline what is required of a Muslim, what is permissible, a middle ground, what is abominable, and what is absolutely prohibited. In one sense, what is required could be said to be that part of the *shar'ia* which is most concerned with the individual, as it directly addresses the Five Pillars of Islam, and therefore the devotional and most highly "religious" part of Islam. In relation to the community of believers, the *shar'ia* seeks to protect the interests of the community as a whole, and the community (*umma*) takes precedence over the individual, who is protected only when his interests are not in conflict with what can be perceived of as the general interest. As a result of centuries of interpretation of these basic concepts in an attempt by Islam to construct a code of law, the *shar'ia* as we see it today provides detailed rules, covering commercial and penal law, marriage and divorce (family law), as well as devotional matters.[20]

In the formative period of Islam, when Muhammad was still alive and guiding the community of believers, the *shar'ia* was a simple thing to understand, because there was no interpretation whatsoever; Muhammad's decisions were absolute, and his authority as the Seal of the Prophets (the last person who will receive divine revelation) meant that any statements made by Muhammad were essentially law. Thus the *hadith* begins. Following the death of Muhammad, believers turned to the *Qur'an* for legal matters, but only between 200 and 500 of the 6,600 verses of the *Qur'an* deal with legal issues, and so the believers turned then to the *hadith*.[21] But the *hadith* obviously dealt only with things that Muhammad had to deal with in his lifetime, and as history progressed, decisions had to be made which Muhammad was never faced with. The *shar'ia* then began to be interpreted by various members of the community of believers, who became scholars of the *Qur'an* and the *hadith*. While it would be counterproductive to reiterate the entire history of Islam in regards to *shar'ia* here, some major points of contention and shifts in the general understanding of the meaning and implementation of *shar'ia* throughout history, particularly *ijtihad*, should be outlined briefly.

THE GATES OF *IJTIHAD*

Throughout the early period of Islam, the definitions of *dar-el-Islam* (the abode of Islam), and *dar-el-harab* (the abode of war), held true for a basic Muslim understanding of the world. There were, of course, travelers and trade caravans, but the *shar'ia* was law only for a small area that had little direct impact on communities outside the boundaries of *dar-el-Islam*. Once the Islamic community began to grow and there were non-Muslim minorities within the boundaries of Islamic territory, the *shar'ia* still was not implemented as legislation per se, but was a code, a way of life, with rulers (caliphs) that dispensed punishment to deviants and dealt with the community of believers. The *shar'ia* continued to be interpreted as events warranted by these *qadis*, because the "questioning, speculative dimension"[22] characterized as *ijtihad* was still widely accepted, and continued to be so until the tenth century. The gates of *ijtihad* began to close slightly earlier than the tenth century though, with the declarations of Muhammad ibn Idris al-Shafii, the father of Islamic law, in the ninth century.

THE FOUR SOURCES OF ISLAMIC LAW

Shar'ia began to become more rigid under the Abbasid dynasty, which in fact came into power on ideals far different that those which resulted in the closing of the gates of *ijtihad* under its rule. Al-Shafii, who taught during the Abbasid dynasty, studied at a variety of legal schools, and eventually began to teach his own understanding of Islamic law. He taught that there were four basic sources for law in Islam: the *Qur'an*, the *sunna*, *ijma* (consensus) of the community, and *qiyas* (analogical reasoning). It is this last point which needs to be emphasized, for there is a crucial difference between analogical difference and independent reasoning. Personal reasoning on the part of the jurists would no longer be acceptable to the community, because it did not have a basis in the *Qur'an* or the *sunna*, the authoritative sources of Islamic doctrine. Therefore, *qadis* (judges) were to restrict themselves to seeking analogous situations in the revelatory sources, from which they would then derive a judgement.[23] This was the first step in the establishment of a stricter *shar'ia*.

THE CLOSING OF THE GATES

Ijtihad, and the speculative ideas of those Muslims attempting to interpret the *shar'ia*—*qadis*, Sufis, poets, intellectuals—resulted in the flowering of Islamic philosophy (*falsafa*) and science, and the Golden Age of Islam under the Abbasids. Under their dynasty the Muslim empire spread, and Arabic language and culture displaced local customs and languages throughout the Middle East, and there was a need for a more uniform code of law. which meant that the law as it existed so far had to be clarified and codified. In order to do this, the *hadiths* came under scrutiny, and an attempt was made to reduce the *hadiths* only to those directly traceable to Muhammad. A community of scholars began to develop—men who were respected in their knowledge of what traditions could be verified —and were supported by the Abbasids. In the end, however, this community of scholars (*ulama*) controlled the caliphate for all intents and purposes. In the West, we tend to think of these *hadith* scholars as theologians, but in the context of Islam, they were really jurists (*fuqaha*)[24] and it is they who closed the gates of *ijtihad* further. Basing their actions on principles laid down by al-Shafii, they began to rely more and more on precedents instead of reasoning, and *taqlid* (imitation) of early scholars became the norm.

As the Abbasid dynasty became corrupt, it also became paranoid, and tried to annihilate the philosophers of Islam, seen as threatening to the regime because of their powers of interpretation which superseded those of the caliph. This tension between the caliphs and the poets, intellectuals and *qadis* was a struggle between the pen and the sword, and in this case the sword won. The tension became construed as a battle between the *shar'ia* and deviants from Islamic principles, and the Abbasid dynasty finally rejected *ijtihad* totally and "propagated an interpretation of *shar'ia* as knowledge revealed in Arabic,"[25] specifically to Muhammad, and gave Islam the legacy of the strict *shar'ia* that Muslims are dealing with today.

In modern times, after the emergence of the nation-state, there have been various attempts in the Muslim world to implement *shar'ia*. As Islam came into contact with the West, and responded to it, the colonialism and secularization of the West threatened many Muslims and there were varying reactions. Secularists looked to the West for inspiration along the lines of church-state separation, advocating a restriction of Islam to the personal sphere, citing a general outmodedness of Islam, and a lack of progressive thinking as contributing to the loss of Islamic power to the West.

At the other end of the spectrum were those who have lately been called "fundamentalists," who said that in fact Islam's loss of power was due to divergence from true Islam, and that a return to a pure Islam and a rejection of Western values and ideas would lead to a restoration of Muslim power and a reclamation of the Golden Age of Islam. Islamic modernists sought a middle ground–an Islamic absorbency of ideas from the West combined with a reformation of Islam itself, with an understanding that Islam would be the focal point in the modernization process, characterizing what could be termed a Muslim response rather than a reaction to the west.[26]

Daniel Pipes, in his essay reconsidering "Fundamentalist Muslims in World Politics," states that in its current incarnation as a complete guide to all walks of life, "The *shar'ia* sets out goals both private and public," and the problem with the public goals is that they "are so lofty that they cannot be met," and therefore full implementation of the *shar'ia* has always eluded Muslims.[27]

This analysis goes on to point out that "fundamentalists" are in fact espousing a radical program that has never been implemented, and thus are false to the their own claim of being traditionalists.

ISLAMIC NATION-STATES

In considering the various Islamic states currently in existence, it should be pointed out that none of them can be considered to have put into place an Islamic state that is any sort of re-creation of a past state. Those that have tried, including Iran and Sudan in particular, have designed regimes which are constantly being reprimanded by the rest of the world for their actions against non-Muslims and their actions such as amputation of the hand in cases of petty theft. Saudi Arabia has also begun to implement stricter *shar'ia* laws recently, but Saudi Arabia is in a unique position in the Muslim World for three reasons: one, it is the historical birthplace of Islam; two, the holiest sites of Islam, Mecca and Medina, are in Saudi Arabia; and three, the economy is bolstered by unmatched oil reserves. This third reason gives Saudi Arabia bit of leeway in the world which other nations wishing to maintain relations with other states wouldn't have. Those states, such as Sudan, which have limited relations with the rest of the world and limited economic resources, are implementing a form of *shar'ia* which is self-destructive, and the West, the East and indeed other Muslims react to with some fear.

In response to statements about Islam in the Western media, and documentaries with biased titles such as the BBC's "The Sword of Allah," the West has developed a basic fear and misunderstanding of Islam, and a major response to questions of what Islam must do is that they [Muslims] must modernize. But those that say this usually mean that Islam must Westernize, and pursue secularization, in the context of a democratic state built along lines of church-state separation. To say that Muslims must modernize is to state an obvious truth, obvious both to the West but also to Muslims, who want Western technology and standards of living, but quite rightly want these benefits on Islamic terms. Many are saying that this is impossible, and that *shar'ia* and the modern nation-state are incompatible, and will always result in totalitarian regimes which will perpetuate human rights abuses and thus will not be able to take their place in the increasingly interdependent world. In a rigid and conservative—what some would call fundamentalist—interpretation of Islam and *shar'ia*, this is quite true, as can be seen in Sudan and in statements made by members of such groups as al-Jihad and other militant Islamic organizations. There is an alternative, however, and it involves an intrinsic Islamic concept. The gates of *ijtihad* must be reopened.

OPENING THE GATES

Ijtihad provides a way for Islam to modernize and yet maintain adherence to *shar'ia*, if the majority of the scholars can see their way clear to reopening the gates of *ijtihad* for all Muslims, not just for scholars, thus in fact returning to an Islamic ideal. Professor Abdol Karim Soroush has opened those gates already, and in his work at the Research Institute for Human Science in Tehran, Iran, is challenging 13 centuries of thinking in his declarations about the religion of Islam.

Using a Western analogy, Soroush is the "Luther" of Islam, and could wind up leading a "Reformation," the political ramifications of which are a separation of church and state in Islam.[28] Soroush's basic statement that has raised eyebrows around the world is that "Islam and democracy are not only compatible, their association is inevitable. In Muslim society, one without the other is not perfect."[29] Soroush is arguing against the kind of rigidity that results in "fundamentalist" interpretations of Islam that reach towards an illusionary past, and justifies his ideas on Islamic theology on solid ground, using language that is Islamic in character—citing two bases for his statements on Islam and democracy:

> "The first pillar is this: To be a true believer,
> one must be free. To become a believer under
> pressure or coercion will not be true belief.
> And this freedom is the basis of democracy.
> The second pillar in Islamic democracy is that
> interpretation of religious texts is always in
> flux. Those interpretations are also influenced
> by the age you live in. So you can never give a
> fixed interpretation."[30]

This means that everyone is entitled to interpret Islam, and this empowerment of ordinary believers can result in a reconciliation between Islam and modernism.

CONCLUSIONS

The *shar'ia* can serve as a basis for legislation, but not for rigid structures that bind everyone to such harshness as *hudud*, the penalty for theft in Sudan, involving public amputation, and abolition of all taxes in favor of a mandatory *zakat*. The role of the *shar'ia* in the Islamic nation-state depends on an understanding of *shar'ia* as comprising underlying principles and ideals, with specifics open to *ijtihad*, as long as any one interpretation does not cater to the interests of the individual above the interests of the *umma*.

There is a role for *shar'ia* in the Islamic nation-state, and it is a crucial one for Muslim theology, but it will take adaptation and compromise to implement a *shar'ia* which can indeed preserve the community of believers. As interaction with the rest of the world becomes essential to a state's economic survival, the *shar'ia* would seem to be the Achilles' Heel for Islam, as Muslims seek to justify the modernization process and still remain true to their heritage. However, an increasing need on the part of Muslims to come to terms with a world in which the barriers between *dar-el-Islam* and *dar-el-harab* are breaking down due to increased communication and transportation technology, combined with the ideas introduced by Abdol Soroush in Iran, can result in a *shar'ia* that serves as the backbone of an Islamic state, allowing its citizens to prosper in the greater world and yet preserve their Islamic legacy.

Al Faruqi, Ismail Raji. *Islam and the Problem of Israel*. London: Islamic Council of Europe, 1980.

Ayubi, Nazib. *Political Islam: Religion and Politics in the Arab World*. London: Routledge, 1991.

Choudhury, G. W. *Islam and the Contemporary World*. London: Indus Thames, 1990.

Clarke, Peter, ed. *The Worlds Religions: Islam*. London: Routledge, 1990.

El-Affendi, Abdelwahab. *Who Needs an Islamic State?* London: Grey Seal, 1991.

El-Affendi, Abdelwahab. *Turabi's Revolution: Islam and Power in Sudan*. London: Grey Seal, 1991.

Esposito, John L. *Islam: The Straight Path*. New York: Oxford University Press, 1991.

_____. *The Islamic Threat: Myth or Reality?* New York: Oxford University Press, 1992.

_____., ed. *Voices of Resurgent Islam*. New York: Oxford University Press, 1983.

Khadduri, Majid. *The Islamic Conception of Justice*. Baltimore: Johns Hopkins University Press, 1984.

Mitchell, Richard P. *The Society of the Muslim Brothers*. New York: Oxford University Press, 1993.

Mernissi, Fatima. *Islam and Democracy: Fear of the Modern World*. London: Addison-Wesley, 1993.

Parry, Glenn E. "The Islamic World: Egypt and Iran," in *Politics and Religion in the Modern World*, ed. George Moyser. London: Routledge, 1991, 97-135.

Pipes, Daniel. "Fundamentalist Muslims in World Politics," in *Secularization and Fundamentalism Reconsidered*, eds. Jeffery K. Hadden and Anson Shupe. New York: Paragon, 1989, 123-132.

Piscatori, James P., ed. *Islam in the Political Process*. Cambridge: Cambridge University Press, 1983.

Warburg, Gabriel R. "The 'Sharia' in Sudan: Implementation and Repercussions, 1983-1989," in *The Middle East Journal* Vol. 44, No. 4 (Autumn 1990): 624-637.

Watt, W. Montgomery. *What is Islam?* London: Longman, 1968.

© K Rayker

The Forgotten Fundamentalism

Hinduism and Nationalism, and the Clash of Religion and Politics in Modern India

INTRODUCTION

In surveying religious resurgence in the modern world and its effect on politics, it is certainly worth taking a close look at India, because up until the introduction of the modern nation-state, "Indian society...many groups of people, who spoke different languages, belonged to different histories and practiced different religions, over a period of hundreds of years learned to live together and interact socially."[31] After the withdrawal of Britain from India, India's continuation of its quest for recognition in the modern world has led to repeated attempts to define itself as a nation-state in the world at large, and ever since the creation of Pakistan, religion has played a tremendous role in the ongoing process of politics in India. Although religion is extremely diverse in India—as the birthplace of Hinduism, Buddhism, Jainism, and Sikhism—an examination of the role of Hinduism, as the largest religion in India, is crucial to an understanding both of Indian politics and, additionally, is important to wider theoretical questions regarding the varying role of religious resurgence in politics in the modern world. Of the approximately 800 million people living in India, 83 percent are Hindu, 11 percent are Muslim, 2.6 percent are Christian, and 1 percent are Sikhs, with smaller communities of Jains, Parsis and Buddhists.[32]

The media has taken the term "fundamentalist" to heart in its discussions about the interaction between religion and politics in today's world, but these discussions have concentrated on Islamic and Christian fundamentalists in the West and the Middle East and ignored the religious revivalism that is surging through much of the Far East. If the media can go so far as to apply the term "fundamentalist" to the vastly different Muslim and Christian movements, it can also certainly apply it to the Hindu militants who are rapidly organizing and deploying across the Indian subcontinent. Not to enter too far into a discussion of the merits of applying the term fundamentalist to various religious movements, it seems fair to say that when the term is used in the popular media, it generally refers to a religious movement which is concerned with expulsion of other religious groups in an attempt to form a society based on the essential truths of one religion, and is not adverse to the idea of using extreme violence and terrorism to achieve those goals. Elements of modern Hindu movements certainly meet these requirements in their attempts to create Hindustan, the Hindu homeland.

It is even more curious for many observers that such elements should arise in Hinduism (relative to the monotheistic religions of the West), as the religion is perceived to be by nature more accepting of differences in beliefs. This is, however, a misconception, and is a bit of modern mythologizing. Hinduism certainly accepts a variety of deities, and has a great diversity within its own structures of yogic ideals, but the basic structures of *karma* ("merit points" gained for spirituality) *dharma* (duty), and sacrifice are quite specific in their ritualization as part of a structured belief system, that pointedly does not include Western yoga practitioners who do the poses for health reasons. Not to digress too far from the role of Hinduism in modern politics, a brief understanding of these concepts is necessary if one is to understand the role Hindus themselves feel they are playing in any context, including the political sphere.

The Indian Hindu has many ways of adhering to his *dharma* and achieving a level of *karma* that allows him to escape from this cyclical universe and move beyond the suffering of this world. These various methods of disciplining oneself are collectively referred to as yoga, a Sanskrit word meaning a discipline or spiritual path, in essence, a method of training designed to lead to integration or union, with "god." Yoga is somewhat of an ambiguous term, but can generally be broken into three main categories for the purpose of discussion.

Loosely defined, these three yogas are *jnana* yoga, *bhakti* yoga and *karma* yoga, and together these three disciplines offer various paths to the same goal, that of *moksa*, enlightenment and release from *karma* (death and rebirth) through a form of sacrifice. The paths vary in difficulty and in methodology, and although each is intrinsically valuable and sacred, there are differences in what might be termed the quality of each, in that those people of higher stations in life are presumed able to follow the more difficult of the yogas, thereby performing a somewhat 'greater' sacrifice.

There is a difficulty, however, in discussing the sacrificial component of these disciplines in English, because the conceptualization of sacrifice for the Hindu is a much wider and deeper understanding of the term than that in Western, secularized culture. In order to more fully understand the role of these yogas as sacrificial in nature, one must first understand the disciplines themselves, which is somewhat impossible, as by their very nature they cannot be understood completely unless one undergoes the disciplines. They can, however, be looked at by examining certain characteristics of each yoga, and then attempting to relate each of these characteristics to sacrifice and in fact to life by means of comparing them to each other.

Jnana yoga, stated simply, is the way to achieve union with "god" through knowledge. Although this knowledge is achieved through knowledge of the *Veda* (the religious texts of the Hindus)—itself achieved through intense Vedic study to the exclusion of all things worldly—the true knowledge is not knowledge in encyclopedic terms, but rather is intuitive knowledge of life itself. In Hindu understanding, this then would mean a realization and acceptance of the oneness of the universe, the overall similarity of reality, and a shift in rationale from a self-centered worldview to a worldview that includes the concept of the human body as a microcosm of the universe—a "universal fractal" in Mandelbrot's terms—and also of the universe as a reflection of the human body, a macrocosm. As the *jnani* yogi reaches the realizations and disciplines the body and mind, the yogi is producing heat in many forms, and this heat is a form of sacrifice. Also, the *jnani* yogi has sacrificed worldly possessions and entertainments to achieve this knowledge.

Karma yoga takes a different approach. Designed for those who are incapable of total renunciation of the world, *karma* yoga allows the practitioner to remain active in daily life, in fact, to become fully active in all possible ways, seeing life itself as a sacrifice. *Karma* yoga could be characterized as a way to reach union with "god" through work. This work includes all normal aspects of being an active participant in daily life, but is also understood as fully practicing one's *dharma*. This concept of *dharma* is central to Indian life, as it dictates everyone's duty from the day they are born, according to their station in life and into what caste they were born. As their caste is in fact a reflection of the current state of their *karma*, by accepting the stage of life which he is at, the *karma* yogi works very hard at being the best he can be at that stage of life, in effect, burning up his old *karma* and creating new *karma*. This act of burning up the old *karma* is seen as sacrificial in nature, and contributes also to the overall accumulation of good *karma* in all of reality, so it is in fact a sacrificial offering, in that it contributes not only to the good of the individual, but also to society and to the universe at large.

Bhakti yoga is sometimes referred to as the way of love. It is so called because this form of yoga essentially consists of incredibly intense worship of "god," which in *bhakti* yoga allows the adherent to conceive of "god" in a way that seems most appropriate to himself. In fact, to the *bhakti* yogi, a true practitioner of the stated goals and aims of Christianity would be seen to be following a path of *bhakti* yoga. This form of yoga dedicates all power to the "god" which is being worshipped, and in return, as the intensity of worship and love radiate out from the heart of the *bhakti* yogi, the "god" will eventually help the yogi escape from *karma*. This process of radiating love can also be seen as a radiation of heat, and therefore sacrifice. A key difference here is that in *bhakti* yogi, or *bhakta*, will not identify with "god," and conceive there to be an underlying unity, but will in fact concentrate on the "otherness" of whatever deity to which that individual is devoting himself.

There is a fourth yoga, that of *raja* yoga, which is that process of physical posturing and meditation that is in effect a series of psycho-physical experiments on the individual's body so often connected with the word "yoga" in Western culture. It is important to understand that in Hindu cosmology, these varying methods of achieving enlightenment, or realization of the *Atman*, are not mutually exclusive. They can in fact be combined and act in concert to lead people down the path which is most suited for their temperament. *Jnana* yoga is thought of as the shortest path, but that is because it is the steepest. The other paths are just as valid, but are perhaps longer, though easier to follow. The Hindu realizes that the importance of each is the act of offering sacrifice in whatever method is most appropriate, for everyone is different, and need to have different ways to reach the same goals.

All of these yogic elements play a role in shaping Indian politics. To give one example, the leaders of the *bhakti* movement of the 15th to 17th centuries consciously avoided politics, but they did so by ridiculing social rituals and social positions. By doing so, they laid the groundwork for today's political movements which argue for social reform, based largely on the spiritual reform called for by adherents of *bhakti* yoga.

Having put forth this framework for understanding the paths a Hindu can follow, it is important to understand that the vast majority of Hindus are actively following *karma* yoga, and perceive themselves to be fulfilling their *dharma* by participating in the daily life of the community. With the introduction of the nation-state by the British, that community has now taken on nationalistic overtones. Many Hindus feel that their community is the nation of India, and one crucial element of their *dharma* is to preserve and protect—through violence if necessary—the Hindu environment, wherein certain practices crucial to achieving *moksa* are left unchanged. One example of this is the practice of *sati*, the burning of a widow. On September 4, 1987, an 18-year old girl committed *sati* (sacrificial suicide) on her husband's funeral pyre. The Indian government, following the British practice of outlawing *sati*, tried to have the *cunari* rite—a rite which bestows sacristy on the *sati* in a sort of consecration of the suicide—suppressed. A whole new organization, Sati Dharma Raksak, was created to protest this governmental action, and 70,000 Indians marched in protest. Eventually, a political party was formed by this organization, which still puts forth candidates and effects the debates surrounding women's issues in India.[33]

The most popular way of understanding religious politics in India is through the idea of communalism. Essentially, this means that groups of like-minded religious people formed political organizations within the secular framework, with policy ideals based on religious motivations of the community from whence originated the political group. While there is no national religious party by name, all religious-derived groups are nationalistic, in that they seek to create a homeland in which laws and legislation are formulated with an understanding of certain religious norms. This holds true for the Muslim League, the Akali Dal ("The Group of Immortals"—the Sikh separatist party), and the various Hindu organizations, including the Rashtriya Swayamsevak Sangh, the Vishwa Hindu Parishad ("The All Hindu Conference"), and the Hindu Mahasabha.

The Hindu Mahasabha is perhaps the Hindu group most affected by the concept of the nation-state, and by the events of partition, which gave the Muslims their own homeland in Pakistan, and the carving up of Punjab, giving the Sikhs an area to call their homeland (Khalistan). The Mahasabha has as its main goal the creation of a completely Hindu state, called Hindustan (Hindu homeland). In such a state, the Mahasabha believes that Hinduism will return its believers to a golden age, in which the main concerns of *dharma* and *karma* will be preeminent in daily life. However, the Mahasabha believes that the homeland in question is all of India, as determined by reference to time periods prior to the Mughal empire. References to Akhand Bharat ("Undivided India") abound in their literature, and they are in fact pledged to attain the goal of

Akhand Bharat by all legitimate means. Those means can be violent, if the occasion necessitates, as was the case in Ayodhya, which serves as an excellent example of how the Mahasabha operates in accordance with its leader's "clarion call" in 1938 to "Hinduize politics and militarize Hinduism."[34]

In 1984, the Vishwa Hindu Parishad (VHP) called for complete Hindu control over all sites related to Hindu worship. Some of these sites, such as the temple at Ayodhya, have had mosques built over them during the period of Muslim rule. After extensive fighting, the government banned both groups from worshipping on the site. Repeated attempts by Hindu militants following the Mahasabha ideals—members of the VHP—to break into the temple resulted in the reopening of the site in 1986. This quickly resulted in further Muslim-Hindu clashes, and the VHP began calling for destruction of the mosque. In 1993, on 6 December, the riots broke out in force. Most Muslims fed the city, but Hindu militants captured the 13 Muslim men, women and children left in the area of Ayodhya and burned them, after destroying all of the Islamic relics in the mosque and looting and burning all Muslim-owned houses and shops in the area. A leader of the VHP, Acharya Dharmendra, was quoted as saying "This is the only way in which Ayodhya can become like the Vatican."[35] Such statements are echoed by Hindu militants around India, as they seek a normal nation for themselves, as they have seen the West set up for Jews and for Muslims.

Incidents such as the one at Ayodhya are innumerable, but it is the motivation that is more important than the events themselves. Each of the Hindus participating in these events sees himself as fulfilling his *dharma*, living the life of *karma* yoga, and pursuing an ideal environment, in which his path to *moksa* will not be hindered by secular governmental laws. Religion and politics are intertwined in India perhaps more than in any other nation, and inasmuch as efforts to force India into the role of a modern nation-state involve secular notions, there are perhaps insurmountable difficulties in attaining that goal. India thrived on communalism until the introduction of nation-state boundaries took away the validity of those communities, and the clash between modern nationalism and Indian communalism will always be expressed in religious terms, as that is the only route of expression available to Hindus who feel that their spiritual progression is threatened by the state. Not all of them, obviously, will join militant groups, but many will, and those that don't join up will probably support the ideas expressed by the groups, without endorsing their actions. Hinduism is indeed "the forgotten fundamentalism" in our Western debates over religious resurgence, forgotten perhaps because in India as nowhere else the actions of the West are at the roots of the current violence.

Amartya Sen, "The Threats to Secular India," in *The New York Review*, April 8, 1993.

Andersen, W. K. and S. D. Damle. *The Brotherhood in Saffron: The Rashtriya Swayamsevak Sangh and Hindu Revivalism*. Boulder, 1987.

Ayoob, Mohammed. "Dateline India: The Deepening Crisis," in *Foreign Policy*, Winter 1991-92.

Barnhart, Joe. "The Incurably Religious Animal," in *Religious Resurgence and Politics in the Contemporary World*, ed. Emile Sahliyeh. New York: State University of New York, 1990, 27-32.

Baxter, Craig. *The Jana Sangh: A Biography of an Indian Political Party*. Philadelphia, 1969.

D'Souza, Dilip. "Crime and Punishment: Combating the Shiv Sena Menace in Bombay," in *Manushi* 78 (1994): 22-6.

Dumont, L. *Religion, Politics and History in India: Collected Papers in Indian Sociology*. The Hague, 1970.

Ghose, S. *Modern Indian Political Thought*. New Delhi, 1984.

Graham, B. D. *Jana Singh and Swatantra: A Profile of the Rightist Parties in India*. Bombay, 1967.

Hardy, Friedhelm. "The Classical Religions of India," in *The Religions of Asia*, ed. Friedhelm Hardy. London: Routledge, 1990, 37-128.

Johnson, David L. *The Religious Roots of Indian Nationalism: Aurobindo's Early Political Thought*. Calcutta: Firma K.L. Mukhopadhyay, 1974.

Juergensmeyer, Mark, ed. *Violence and the Sacred in the Modern World*. London: Frank Cass, 1991.

Kishwar, Madhu. "Criminalisation of Politics," *Manushi* 79 (1994): 7-9.

Nandy, Ashish. "An Extract From 'An Anti-Secularist Manifesto'," *Manushi* (1994): 49.

Towards New Images of Peace

The Failure of Just-War Doctrine

and its Related Imagery

In the course of history, actions involving the security of organizations—tribes, regional alliances, empires, nations, nation-states—have resulted in war, with peace being the "desired" outcome. In this process of war and peace, humans have set about justifying their actions, and in that justification had to reconcile their actions fundamentally with their religious ideals. When speaking of theories of war and peace, it must be understood that at the religious/cultural level, these theories can better be spoken of as images, cultural images, which allow the relatively uneducated to participate in the culture-wide justification of a specific action.

FOUR THEORIES OF WAR AND PEACE

In the United States, these justifications have followed the history of Christian doctrines regarding war, and therefore, images of war and peace in the United States have tended to fall under one of the following four top-level theories of war and peace: Holy War, Just War, Christian humanism, and pacifism, with second-layer mini-images developed beneath them. The United States, and by extension, the Western world, has successfully worked under a combination of these movements, putting forth mini-images such as apocalypticism and balance of power underneath the major images. In the final analysis however, these images eventually fail at several levels in achieving the goal of a lasting peace, and it is time for a new image to be put forth.

The four top-level theories have been generally successful within the boundaries of the United States, although pacifism has been primarily a background movement, or relegated to very religious factions. The majority of United States citizens feel the need to reconcile themselves with the Christian faith, but also feel the need to keep that reconciliation relatively private, reflecting the cultural necessity in the United States of separating religion from day-to-day life, and so pacifism, which has very strong roots deep in the Christian faith, has been primarily unsuccessful in the United States. Pacifism has not played a role in the United States' international actions, although it has met with some success internally, as in the Civil Rights movement headed by the Rev. Dr. Martin Luther King. Pacifism has been partially successful in other countries and religions, particularly where it was characterized as the theory of *ahimsa*, or non-violence, from the Jain, Hindu and Buddhist traditions. It was put forth and used effectively by Mohandas Ghandi in both South Africa and, to a much greater degree, in India. The problem with non-violence as an image is that it carries some connotations of a negative nature in the United States. Pacifists have been looked at in derogatory terms in the United States, particularly as draft dodgers, although this is changing somewhat with regards to Vietnam and Bill Clinton. The idea of pacifism has always been a minority opinion in the United States, and from a religious standpoint, those religions advocating pacifism such as the Quakers and the Mennonites have always had relatively small communities. The other three theories have all been used, often in conjunction with one another, to justify the United States' actions in the international arena, particularly the Just War doctrine.

It is difficult to separate Holy War from Just War in the United States, because the policies of the United States are inextricably bound up in Christianity—resulting in the success of the essentially Christian Just War doctrine. Although the United States is a secular state, it is secular in a very peculiar way; the country is understood at the cultural level in terms of images such as the "City on the Hill," founded as the "New Jerusalem," and as the "Redeemer Nation" in the world. The policies of the United States in times of war are therefore inherently the actions of a country at Holy War, as it is literally impossible for the United States to be involved in anything but a Holy War, and it is with this image that the initial involvement in the war is understood at the cultural image level. The specific incidents of the war are then discussed under Just War auspices, and after the war the United States follows the Christian humanist approach in cleaning up. All three of these images have been successful in the United States, at least until Vietnam, where they finally began to fray.

These images were, however, destined to fail eventually. None of these images take into account diversity of religion and values, and it is obvious that as the world becomes increasingly interdependent, Christianity can no longer be the sole source of religious images of war and peace. However, it is also obvious that religious revivalism—Christian fundamentalists in the United States, Islamic and Judaic revivalism in the Middle East —must also be accounted for in any new image of war and peace in the United States and in the international community. More importantly, none of these images have a realistic path to a lasting peace. Holy War implies eschatology, as a war won by Christianity would result in the complete destruction of evil, ushering in the kingdom of God. Just War is involved in combating chaos, and preserving or repairing firm borders (physical, national, behavioral) to keep out chaos. However, this means that chaos is forever just outside the borders and the best result of a war is to re-establish order—create new balance of power—but all results are finite and temporary. Peace means simply preparing for the next war as you keep the balance of power as stable as possible.

Christian humanism fails in its basic understanding of humanity, in that it has at its core a belief that humans are rational and perfectible; therefore, until that state of perfection is achieved by all humans, conditions exist for war, and a lasting peace is not possible. Any successful image must take into account that the simple existence of diverse value systems will result in the creation of conflict, but Christian humanism automatically elevates that conflict to the status of war and therefore has no path towards lasting peace. Pacifism has a similar failing, in that this image has at its core an idea of peace as a community living according to Christ's teachings, recreating the "golden age" of early Christianity, showing perfect love expressed through absolute nonviolence, and this example will theoretically gradually influence the world to move toward nonviolence. Apart from its reliance on unsubstantiated and romantic views of early Christianity, pacifism fails because it also assumes that a complete lack of conflict is a reality to be achieved, and bases that assumption on a perception of humans as being able to operate in a totally selfless fashion, ignoring the realities of diversity in an increasingly interconnected world. So we see that although these images and the images put forth under their auspices have met with limited success, they were destined to fail. It is clear that the United States, as the only remaining superpower, needs a new image of war and peace, as indeed does the Western world and the rest of the world at large.

In order to be successful, a new theory of war and peace—or in religious terms, a new image of peace—must do two things. First, it must guide the nation's policies away from war and toward peace. Second, it must have broad popular appeal so that political leaders will adopt it and act on it. Many images have been put forth by various writers, social philosophers, religious leaders, scientists and people concerned about the proliferation of violence, but few of these meet both of the above mentioned criteria. Most, if not all, meet at least the first one, that of guiding the nation away from war, but the problem is in meeting the second criteria; proposing an image of peace that is popular in the United States is much more difficult than simply theorizing about the end of war as a political entity.

The images used in the United States to promote peace for the past 200 years have been remarkably successful, in that the United States has had basic peace within its borders since the Civil War and no real attack on the country since perhaps the War of 1812, other than the attack on Pearl Harbor which took place in Hawaii, sufficiently distant from the greater United States as to not have dramatic impact on the greater cultural image of the country as a haven. In general, United States citizens accept the images which have been promulgated throughout the history of the country, so the problem with new images of peace is not only meeting the two criteria already mentioned. Any new images of peace must also overcome the previous images; domestic tranquillity, liberal internationalism, apocalypticism, and balance of power images have served the United States well in its attempt to get beyond the four major images, but none of them have been truly successful as they do not lead towards a lasting peace. United States citizens have had an essentially tranquil country (although urban warfare is becoming an issue, it is seen primarily as a class issue, not a general state of action) and as far as international involvement, US citizens see themselves as having not been the initiators of any war; the United States has stepped into international conflicts under the burden of the "redeemer nation" image. However, the United States has been to war, and there is no denying that the wars it has been involved in have not resulted in a permanent peace, which most US citizens would say is the eventual goal. The United States could not move on to a new era of peace without having passed through these stages in its national understanding of peace, but where does it go now, and how does it get there?

Given the criteria of moving United States policy away from war and towards peace and broad public appeal for new images of peace, there are several images that could be put forth in the United States that would successfully move the US towards a more peaceful existence. The first image that would be successful at promoting peace in the context of American ideology would be agreement on process. Such an image would provide a basis for other images to work. One such image is that of nuclear abolition, which would require agreement on many sides in the United States, and internationally as well, if it is to have a global effect. Another such image would be one of a new world order, not exactly in former President George Bush's terms, but in terms of a world based on the precepts of conflict resolution. Another image, in the tradition of "-isms," would be a modification of Christian humanism, resulting in what might be called pluralist humanitarianism, an image of peace that would encompass the ideas of human rights, human dignity, and responsible individualism, without excluding people of other religious traditions and perhaps more importantly, without evoking images of the "religious right" with its Christian fundamentalists, and also without putting forth Western humanism which is rejected by Islamic movements worldwide.

The image of nuclear abolition is one image of peace which is of particular relevance since the end of the Cold War and the subsequent downfall of the Soviet Union and East Germany. As long as the bomb exists, it will have a determinative and destructive influence on the way we talk, think and act about everything else in the world. The existence of nuclear weaponry has done more than any other singular item or construct to shape the United States' current image of peace. That image is one based on apocalypse management, which came out of the Eisenhower era and was solidified under Reagan, whose declarations of "winning a nuclear war" led to the increased use of nuclear weapons as symbolic images of stability.

The idea of nuclear abolition would be perhaps the most powerful new image of peace, as it would be the strongest possible source and symbol of rejecting the discourse of stability and apocalypse management. The way nuclear imagery is currently used, continued non-proliferation treaties and nuclear freezes do little to eliminate the currently maintained weapons. Thus the existence of the weapons and the motions to keep them from being used provide a constant means of balancing power in the world. The weapons are the most widely recognized instrument of war, and to remove them would certainly fulfill the first criteria, that of directing American policy away from and towards peace. Nuclear abolition also meets the second criteria, as it merely perpetuates an already accepted idea; America has consistently led the way in super-power negotiations for nuclear non-proliferation. Abolition is merely the next logical step. In fact, in the early 1950s, when the US was not the only owner of atomic weaponry but still far in advance of even the Soviet Union in terms of possession amounts, there were at least three times—Korea, 1953; Indochina, 1954; Taiwan Strait, 1954–55—when atomic weaponry was considered but decided against by the United States. If American policy-makers simply continue what they have been doing, the logical step is abolition, and America would once again be able to lead the rest of the world down the path of rationality, an image which would sit well with US citizens adhering to their "redeemer nation" image. The destroying of the weapons alone would not suffice, however, as the removal of these weapons would then cause a space to open up in national and international discourse that would then have to be filled with some alternative means of interaction among nations. That space would be available to be filled with such constructs as conflict resolution.

If conflict resolution is to become a viable image of peace, it must first be considered a goal, not a process. The means of achieving that goal is arbitration, not mediation, which are two separate processes. In arbitration, the decision of the arbiter is final, and enforceable if the process and the unknown result are agreed upon. In mediation, the mediator (serving a different role than an arbiter) merely facilitates discussion, but does not involve him/herself in the final agreement. When an agreement is reached after mediation, the parties enter into a contractual agreement, but no decision or action is forced upon them. Thus, the parties could then possibly end up in conflict once again. Therefore, in order for conflict resolution to work, the optimum means of achieving resolution would be arbitration. As far as meeting the criteria, the goal of conflict resolution via these two processes is already becoming an accepted means of dealing with conflict in the United States, primarily for economic reasons. As the public becomes more and more concerned about the eventual use of each tax dollar, military spending is coming under more scrutiny and more attack. To persuade the American public that arbitration in the international arena is more cost effective would be an easy task, and there is no doubt that it would lead the United States away from war and towards peace.

If arbitration is to be useful in international situations, several key issues must first be resolved. First, there must be an arbiter. In an ideal world, any nation or party could act as arbiter, but as this is merely a discussion of the first possible steps to peace from a United States perspective, the reality is that such an arbiter must be as impartial as possible, and no nation-state could be conceived as such. The closest possible thing to an impartial arbiter would be the United Nations.

This, of course, is where a new world order concept would have to be recognized and put into motion. The United Nations which would fulfill such a role would truly have to be a completely worldwide organization, with all nations as members, and would itself have to be carefully cognizant of issues such as religious identity. In a world where the United Nations would serve as arbiter, the member nations would also have to be much more fully aware of the diversity among peoples, and more than that, would have to be accepting of that diversity. Such ideas would also involve an acceptance of some levels of conflict that need not escalate into violence. In order for this to succeed, however, there has to be a paradigm shift in the understanding of what peace actually constitutes. Quite simply, there needs to be an understanding by all parties that creation–seen in this context as the creation of peace–involves conflict, but rather than characterizing it as conflict, why not characterize the process undergone in conflict resolution simply as a creative struggle? (This type of characterization can be seen in many feminist writings, which use birth as an example of this kind of creative struggle.) If all parties are in agreement as to the process, then the result is not as significant, and there need not be conflict over that result.

Given the acceptance of diversity on a national, international and organizational plane, the member nations would have to agree on the process of arbitration itself before any positive results could be forthcoming. But for there to be any change in the war and peace processes in the world, there must first be widespread agreement on an ideal of a process by which peace might be realized. The ideal of peace is too diverse itself for it to be a successful image. If people were encouraged simply to imagine peace, the various results would themselves be in conflict and would not lead to any peace at all. If, however, people were to imagine a process by which resolution is achieved without violent conflict, the end result would be peace, without that being the stated goal. There is a common statement among prison program inmates that the reason they are there is not because they planned to be there, but because they didn't have a plan to stay out. This same kind of logic needs to be applied to peace imagery. It is not that we need to plan to have peace, we need to actively concern ourselves with not having war, opening a space in international relations, and then filling that space with alternative processes. Peace will naturally follow.

These ideas are all predicated on the last image of peace in this discussion, and that is the one labeled "pluralist humanitarianism." Christianity is no longer the best basis for broad popular appeal. Although the President of the United States still calls on God to bless the nation, the rise of the "religious right" and what are (often incorrectly) perceived of as its strong biases against ethnic, sexual and religious diversity has done much to limit the power of Christianity to draw diverse groups of people together in the United States. Regardless of the "religious right," the post-modern trend has been away from religion, in the sense that secularization is seen to be an inevitable part of modernization. But secularism has two possible connotations: one is a rejection of religion; the second is an acceptance of deliberate church/state separation. Therefore, to say that a conception of pluralist humanitarianism is an essential component of new images is emphatically not to say that religion must be ignored in the formulation of a new image of war and peace, but that for a new image to truly have broad popular appeal, it must get beyond religious ideals without rejecting them. This is possible, as all religions have at their foundational levels an emphasis on the individual's actions.

Wrapped in the Christian foundation is the notion of rugged individualism, and although some might argue the efficacy of the term "rugged," the idea of individualism does connote responsibility, and it is really here that any successful images of peace must begin. All societies, nations, organizations and institutions are ultimately made up of individuals, and it is those individuals who must decide to subscribe to new images of peace. The recognition of the individual responsibility includes the recognition of all individuals, and the rights of those individuals as well as their responsibility. As the *Universal Declaration of Human Rights* points out in its first article, "All human beings are born free and equal in dignity and rights. They are endowed with reason and conscience and should act towards one another in brotherhood." (*Universal Declaration of Human Rights*. Adopted by UN GA Res. 217(III) of 10 December 1948 (UN GAOR 3(I)).) Such an idea should be an easy one for Americans to use as an acceptable image of peace, as it is based on their own Constitution. From the standpoint of leading US policy towards peace, it is hard to see how anyone could use the idea of brotherhood as a prelude to war. As far as the criteria of broad popular appeal, it is proof—for those who wish it—of the United States of America leading the way once again, something the politicians can really sink their teeth into, although this time the way is not that of capitalism or democracy, but the path of peace.

If any of these images of peace are to be successful, however, they must all be implemented. Just one new image of peace is insufficient to begin any radical change in the US view of war and peace. Beginning with a change on the individual level towards a more humanitarian lifestyle, and continuing with these other ideas, the images of peace discussed here have at least the "best" chance of success.

Islam

The Greening of Mohammed

Towards an Understanding of

Islam and the Environment

To claim knowledge of what Islam "thinks" or "says" about any subject is at least in part an impossibility, as there are many variations of Islam, and indeed, in a literal—some would say "liberal"—interpretation of the Islamic concept of *ijtihad* and the attempt of Islam to spread across disparate cultures there cannot help but be multiple interpretations of Islam. However, it is possible to seek an understanding of what those Muslims who are talking and thinking about a subject are in fact basing their statements on, and such is the point of this essay: that is, to gain an understanding of what those Muslims concerned about the environment are saying and how they arrive at their conclusions in an Islamic context, both for a greater understanding of how the world might present a combined front to the environmental problem, and—because of the mutual concern of the subject matter—the subject itself perhaps presents a new opportunity to explore the issue of Christian (Western)-Muslim relations.

In our world of rapidly changing borders, cross-cultural business dealings and globalization, perhaps the most global of all concerns facing the emerging world order is the environment. Security has long been a concern of nation-states, but the environment is the first global security concern. "In the global context, true security...depends on global cooperation to ensure a sustainable biological environment."[36] Yet even with mounting evidence of the destruction of the environment, relatively little is being done to combat the degeneration of our planet. One reason for this hesitance to mount a worldwide campaign for the environment is the continuing misunderstandings among nations and cultures, not the least of which is the continuing ignorance and fear regarding Islam that prevails in many Western areas. A perfect example of this lack of understanding can be seen in President Bill Clinton's remarks immediately following the bombing of the Oklahoma Federal Building in 1995: "Make no mistake, this is an attack against America and the way we live!" implying quite obviously that the assumed attackers were of Middle-Eastern origin with additional statements regarding the status of Muslims undergoing a trial for the New York City bombing incident a year and half earlier. Continued rhetoric from The White House and other organizations speculating on the perpetrators attempted to whip up fear towards Muslims as they pointed a finger of blame towards as yet unknown Islamic radical terrorists, and media reports of searches for Middle Eastern men mounted. Of course, the truth was that an American self-styled patriot was responsible, but the implications of the early statements and whispers in America underscore the fact that "Islam" still strikes a chord of fear in many Western hearts and minds. Clearly, there is a need for greater understanding of Islamic ideals in many areas, and as the environment affects us all, it is perhaps an excellent beginning point.

Since environmental issues entered into greater discourse in the 1970s, Islam, along with all religions, has sought within itself for ideological justifications for environmental positions. As a religion in the Christian and Judaic traditions, Islam has to fight the same criticisms that its male oriented belief structure with its judgmental male god and its rejection of earlier "Mother Earth" traditions is inherently anti-ecological. To counter this, both Christian and Muslim theologians have developed the concept of vice-regency or stewardship over the earth to a higher degree, and in their more offensive moments, have pointed that the Eastern traditions of Buddhism, Hinduism and Taoism are not as ecologically aware as might initially be supposed, as their concepts of illusionary reality do not lead towards proactive care of the environment.[37] Into this discourse environmentally-concerned Muslims must introduce a framework for ecology— not an easy task, as in Islam this means reshaping basic ideas regarding man's place and function in the world to address sustainable development issues at a time when Islam is attempting to come to terms with development and modernization itself.

It must first be understood that whenever elements in Islam attempt to define or redefine a subject, that definition must be undertaken in the context of the *shar'ia*, literally the "source of water," and thus the source of life for Muslims worldwide. The *shar'ia* is more than a code of laws, and more than an ethical framework—although it embodies both—and any attempt on the part of Muslims to introduce an idea into the greater Islamic consciousness must first be reconciled with the *shar'ia*. Such is the case with environmentalism, which for Muslims must be framed in terms of ethics, and thus encapsulated within the *shar'ia's* five categories of actions: Obligatory (*wajib*); devotional/ ethical (*mandub*); permissible (*mubah*); abominable (*makruh*); and prohibited (*haram*).[38] Islamic environmental ethics, as Mawil Izzi Deen and others have attempted to frame it, seem to fit into the category of *makruh*, as actions which Muslims are discouraged from performing on the basis of their ethical virtues.

Some of the Muslim scholars attempting to shape an Islamic response to the environmental crisis and place actions committed by Muslims within this hierarchy are Mawil Izzi Deen[39], similar to other Islamic writers such as Ziauddin Sardar[40] and Syed Hossein Nasr[41]. Nasr is perhaps most important in that his 1968 book provides a starting point for new Islamic ideas about the earth, and the idea of nature as a path to the sacred. The book takes as its starting point that Islam has ecological credentials in its sacred literature and in fact states that Islam can be seen as the true answer to ecological religions, in that it provides a perfect medium between Western and Eastern religions. Expanding on this idea, Nasr goes on to point out that man and nature cannot be separated in Islam, and that humanity has been appointed as caliph (*khalifa*) over the earth.[42] Nasr also briefly uses the concept of *tawhid*, or unity, but quickly moves onto other topics, as subsequent Muslim writers also have done. But in the final analysis, Derek Wall is correct to say that in Nasr's view, the earth itself is not sacred, but merely serves as an appropriate path to what is sacred, which is beyond the known world[43], but the main downfall of using Nasr in the Islamic environmental movement is his lack of providing contextual actions which should be encouraged in the protection of the environment, probably more a reflection of the time in which he was writing, than upon Nasr himself.

Mawil Izzi Deen takes up the cause effectively, but seems to focus not on actions which should be performed, but on those which should not, giving the example of elephant poaching as an abominable action. "Although a Muslim poacher may be able to shoot elephants and avoid game wardens, if a framework based on Islamic principles for the protection of the environment has been published, he knows that he will not be able to avoid the ever-watchful divine Warden."[44] An interesting comparison with Western green movements and ecological awareness should be pointed out here, in that this characterization of environmental ethics is somewhat reactive, a concept which has not proved to be a very complete answer in the West, where proactive environmental ethical actions such as recycling have been much more successful in increasing ecological awareness. Izzi Deen does go on to say, however, that "humans must intervene in order to protect the earth," but he gives no proactive examples, and furthermore he states that the position taken above is "the Islamic position with regard to the environment."[45]

One has to wonder here who Izzi Deen considers his audience to be in his essay, "Islamic Environmental Ethics, Law, and Society," as he seems to be framing an argument both to convince Western readers of the legitimacy and non-threatening stance of the concept of the *shar'ia*, as well as trying to sway Islamic Westerners that a call to be ecologically aware exists in the *Qur'an*. By splitting his argument in this way, he opens the door for the same critical remarks levied at Christian eco-theologists, who are said to be finding truths which simply are not there, in their reinterpretations and debates on Biblical passages such as "Let us make man in our own image, in our likeness, and let them rule over the fish of the sea and the birds of the air, over the livestock, and over all the creatures that move along the ground."[46] It is this quotation from the *Bible* which has been argued to mean a variety of different things in regards to eco-theology, both that the earth is here for man to do with as he wishes, and conversely that man is given the earth to be vice-regent over, caring for it and nurturing it as a farmer cares for the land. Izzi Deen uses this concept in his essay as well, stating that "Humans are not the owners, but the maintainers of the due balance and measure which God provided for them and the animals that live with them," and that "God entrusted humans with the duty of vice-regency, a duty so onerous and burdensome that no other creature would accept it," backing up these statements with Qur'anic quotes.[47] He also opens the door for those who would say that in his attempts to reconcile Western readers to *shar'ia's* ideas of law and ethics, he is attempting to validate the conceptual underpinnings of those whom the West and the Western media in particular have portrayed as "Islamic fundamentalists." Although he does make a brief attempt to discuss how the *shar'ia* plays a role in the life of every Muslim, he fails to make a clear argument for his Western readers of how the *shar'ia* can continue to play a key role in modern Islam as it attempts to come to terms with democratization, Westernization, and modernization. While not the point of this essay, it seems that the concept of Islamic eco-theology cannot be introduced into the Western environmental discussion without first establishing its credentials by answering the question of the integration of *shar'ia* with post-modernity, especially in arguments devoted to the differences between law and ethics in Western ideologies as compared to Islam; while he must make his argument acceptable to the West, he must also make it palatable to Muslims.

Although Mawil Izzi Deen strives to make clear that the Islamic environmental effort cannot succeed based on legalities —"an imported, alien law cannot work because...it cannot be made morally binding upon Muslims"[48]—he seems to be implying that environmental awareness must be imparted to Muslims as strict injunctions stating that which should not be done for fear of retribution. True, the retribution is divine, but because of the mingling of legal rules and ethical principles in the *shar'ia*, the basis is still much closer to a legally-derived set of environmental laws in the West than it is to a purely ethical framework. This does not, however, mean that such a framework is or will be any less successful in curbing the destruction of the earth within their context. It does mean that while Izzi Deen makes the claim that the Prophet Mohammed was environmentally aware and that the *Qur'an* has much to say on the topic of ecology, he also must prove that he and other Muslims concerned with the environment are not simply framing a Western response to the ecological crisis by finding

Qur'anic sources and quotes from the *Hadith* which support ideas already in place in the West, and tread a fine line—perhaps an impossible one to tread within the confines of a single essay.

In attempting to frame an Islamic eco-theology, Izzi Deen and others must place Islam definitively both within the context of the environmental movement and also within the context of the specifically religious environmental movement. At one extreme of the religious aspect of the movement are the Jain's who could be said to be "deep ecologists" in their beliefs that all forms of life should be protected forever. At the other end are a variety of Christian, Jewish and other religious eco-theologists who could be classified as "environmentalists," in that they are concerned about the environment, with that concern based on interaction with the environment but without making substantial changes to their lifestyles. The "green" category, comprised of those who could be said to making changes to their lifestyle specifically because of the environmental repercussions of the modern life, seems to be predominantly secular, and is exemplified in the Green Parties of Europe. Environmentally concerned Muslims are placing Islam in the category of "ecologists," as those who are trying to maintain a balance in the world. It is curious that more emphasis therefore is not placed on the concept of *tawhid* in Islamic environmental discourse, as this idea of unity encompasses the idea of striking a balance in all things, both earthly and spiritual. Even in "The Islamic Declaration on Nature," formulated as part of the *Assisi Declarations on Faith and Nature*, *tawhid* is mentioned only in passing, and the emphasis is placed on humanity's role as a "vice-regent or trustee of God" (a *khalifa*).[49] This lack of emphasis on *tawhid* perhaps reflects a concern within the Islamic environmental movement with radical Islam, whose statements on *tawhid* still reflect a *dar-el-harab* and *dar-el-Islam* bifocal view of the world, dividing all the earth and its citizens into those living in the "abode of Islam" and those living in the "abode of war" with *tawhid* essentially impossible with this direct barrier to earthly realization of the *umma*.

In order to frame Islam and Muslims as "ecologists," eight specific ideas have been formulated by Muslims as the summation of the legal and ethical (*shar'ia*-derived) reasons for protection of the environment. Each idea is justified in the context of the *Qur'an*, after which, presumably, specific nation-state laws can be drafted based upon these ideas in order to conserve the environment.

The first reason for conserving the environment in Islam is rather similar to the primary reason in Christian and Jewish eco-theology—that the earth and all of creation is the most powerful and most concrete sign of the Creator, and is therefore deemed to be unique and should be protected, irrespective of any human needs or desires to reap excessive benefits from the Earth.[50] This is also quite close in its basic form to the position taken by the United Nations, in its environment resolution, which proclaims that nature and the world is worthy of respect because it is unique, regardless of its worth to humans.

The second Islamic reason for protecting the environment is a continuation of the first, which is that each and every "component part" of nature, including trees, stones, rivers, etc.

are all praising Allah by their very existence. The form of their praise cannot be understood by humans, but the fact of their existence is not simply that they are signs of the Creator, but are indeed singing praises to the Creator. This idea can also be seen in Jain ideas of the value of both animate and inanimate objects in combining to produce harmony in the universe.

The third reason given by Islamic ecologists for protecting the environment is in fact an idea that bears remarkable similarity to many Western ideas, including that of natural law. It is essentially the idea that there are laws of nature designed by God to ensure the continuity of existence, and to break any of these laws is to defy God, obviously an action deemed to be *makruh*. Although Izzi Deen states that Islamic ideas of what is legal and what is not cannot be linked with humanistic philosophy-derived ideas of law, it would seem that this third reason, and its relationship with the ideas of natural law, is also related to what Thomas Aquinas would term "Eternal Law," in that it derives mainly from revelation, and is in fact the embodiment of God's will and justice. For how else can those eternal truths characterized as the laws of God be understood except through revelation?

The fourth reason given for Islamic ecology is that the humanity is not the only community living in the world. Both Qur'anic passages and statements of Mohammed can be found which support the idea that although humans are at the top of the living hierarchy, being made in God's own image, this does not mean that humans have the right to treat animals with derision, for they too are "people" in their own right.

Mohammed, similar to Christian and Judaic prophets, remarks upon the value of kindness to animals, as Izzi Deen demonstrates by quoting the statement "For [charity shown to] each creature that has a wet heart there is a reward,"[51] as an example of Mohammed's concern for all living creatures.

Although *tawhid* does not seem to play as a large a role in Islamic environmental ethics as one would suspect, another key aspect of Muslim theology does play a role in the fifth reason for Muslims to be concerned about the environment. The concept of justice (*'adl*) and the related idea of equity (*ihsan*) are understood to be important in that all relationships are based on these principles, including relationships between humans, between humans and animals, humans and the environment, and indeed between humans and creation itself. Thus, more than maintenance of balance—the sixth reason—is needed, that balance must furthermore be just. Although closely intertwined, these are indeed two separate issues for the Muslim, who for instance might wish to maintain balance in spiritual concerns by performing a sacrifice, but must do it sparing as much suffering to the animal as possible, thus maintaining justice as well.

This idea of balance forms the essence of the sixth reason given by Muslim eco-theologians for Islamic environmental ethics. Balance in the universe is implicit; it is in balance by virtue of being a creation of God. That balance becomes explicit when it is understood that humans have the responsibility of preserving that balance in their daily lives, both spiritually and physically. To promote environmental ideas, preservation of ecological balance must be encouraged, and be understood in an Islamic context to be an act of worship.

The seventh reason formulated by these environmentally concerned Muslims is based on Islamic ideas of time and space, with regards to humanity. Essentially, this is the idea that the earth must be preserved for future generations, an argument in line with many secular environmentalists, who are also pointing out that the earth is rapidly being changed by humanity, more rapidly in the past 30 years than in the rest of human history, and that unchecked development will ruin the environment for future generations. In Islam, the idea is put forth in the context of the universe having been created a certain way by Allah, and that creation should remain constant for all time, and for all people.

The eighth and final reason for Muslims to become environmentally conscious is that humans are unique in being responsible for becoming aware of their duty to creation, as *khalifa*, or vice-regents. Here there is direct Qur'anic text which supports this idea, as there is in the Old Testament. In the *Qur'an*, it is Allah who says to his angels that he "will create a vice-regent on Earth." Allah then created Adam, and told him of the nature of all things, including the angels, to whom Adam then explained their natures, after which he was accepted to be a knowledgeable vice-regent, created by Allah for this task.[52]

Based on these eight reasons, an ethical framework is proposed by Izzi Deen for Muslims to judge their actions related to the environment, and furthermore base legislation upon the basis of that framework. Thus is law created that is morally binding upon Muslims, because it is based on a principle that is unshakable. In the case of Saudi Arabia and the whole of the Middle East, this seems to be a contradictory process–one perhaps inherently doomed to failure–as the nation-states of the Middle East depend upon their economies for their place in the international order, and those economies are primarily based on the most environmentally devastating modern practice: oil production. Any attempt on the part of these countries to legislate environmental codes is essentially hypocritical, but this issue is not being addressed within the Islamic world at this time. This is not to demean the attempt of concerned Muslims to formulate and implement a specifically Islamic ethic on ecological concerns. Such an attempt is crucial to alleviating the environment crisis worldwide, as are similar attempts in other religious traditions, and inter-religious dialogue towards that goal is at least as important.

As the five billion-plus members of the human race try to reconcile themselves to a rapidly vanishing world, the direction that religious leaders give in combating ecological problems is vital; Islamic scholars and eco-theologians are making their contribution to the war against ourselves and our selfish nature. What is of increasing concern is that disparate movements become synchronized, so that a coordinated effort to curb environmental degradation can be made. To that end, it would seem that Muslims have some issues to resolve regarding the image of radical Islam that permeates Western thought, and it is in that area that further research and writing is warranted on both sides of the religious gulf, and the environmental issues provide a perfect context for that discourse.

The Spirit of Glasnost

Religion and Spirituality in the

Collapse of the Soviet Union

In any society which undergoes a major revolution, there are dozens if not hundreds of factors which bring the tension in the country to the brink of overthrowing its government. Societies which have been organized around the theme of repression offer all sorts of reasons why people finally revolt. Various groups of people, including intellectuals, workers and even some elite members of a society must have some common ground before they can band together to throw off the yoke of repression. Religion may be the strongest of these bonds, as it crosses class boundaries more easily than any other social trait. To paraphrase Paul Tillich, the dynamics of religion are mankind's ultimate concern.[53] When a government suppresses religion, it takes a very dangerous step, for the adherents of religion are adamant about their faith, and even members of different faiths will often proclaim the rights of other religious groups across all types of boundaries, including national, for "The life and death struggle of rebellious autonomy with the powers of religious suppression has left a deep scar in the 'collective unconscious.'"[54]

A political system such as communism has at heart many difficulties in maintaining its structure, but one of the most troublesome is its denial of a god and a religion organized around that deity. In the final revolution of the Soviet Union, there was not much talk about religion, but nonetheless the role played by religion in laying the foundations of dissidence is an enormous one, and such was the role religion played in the Soviet Union. Olga Kerkina, writing in the city of Tver, writes "The church was the base of support...Yet, October 1917 came, and since then 77 years have passed...One thing is doubtless: a terrible substitution took place, instead of trust in God we started trusting in communism. To be more exact, they tried to make Russian people absolute non believers. This is impossible, since faith is an integral part of the Russian soul."[55]

The Soviet Union has been the center of communism for many decades, and in that communist society, the people lived without the benefits of free religion. Free religion is one of the treasures of the Western world, and a facet of life which keeps many people sane. In free religion, members of various faiths are permitted to worship in any manner they choose, while continuing participation in other areas of life, i.e., politics, job markets, and home life. A country which permits this exchange of religious ideas can be said to have a subculture, or a religious society. Even though Russia was under autocratic rule for centuries prior to communism, such a religious society did exist in Russia. In fact, in Christianity, Russia had an immensely strong religious orientation. The Orthodox churches of Eastern Europe had for centuries a tradition which claimed that Moscow was equal to, if not greater than, Constantine's New and Second Rome, Constantinople. With the founding of St. Petersburg by Peter the Great, Orthodoxy had a true seat, even after Peter the Great himself rejected the religion. For many years Russia was the sole proponent of Orthodoxy, and was thus a great source of religious strength to members of its faith worldwide, and a great source of pride to the believers within the nation.[56]

For the years dominated by Leninism and Stalinism, the Soviet government sought to recreate the Soviet mind, forming a culture bereft of a religious society. "For seventy years a state, for the first time in history, attempted to eradicate all concept of God from society. In 1988, Soviet leaders not only realized they had failed, but they put the process into reverse."[57] Where does the impetus for this change originate? Mikhail Gorbachev, the man at the center of the changes, must be looked to for this answer. But in tracing the progress of church *perestroika* in the Soviet Union, one must look not only at Mr. Gorbachev today, one must spend some time examining the history of religion and religious persecution in the USSR, the early influences on Mr. Gorbachev, and the past and present Soviet political make-up.

Religious persecution in the Soviet Union began under Vladimir Lenin, in the early 1900s. Lenin began his reign of terror by appropriating all of the moneys of the church in an unprecedented attack on religion. In a letter dated March 19, 1922, Lenin demanded that the most merciless measures be taken to crush all opposition to the proposed confiscation of church treasures. The letter continued, saying "We must appropriate at all costs this source of several millions of gold rubles, while suppressing resistance so brutally that they [the clergy] will remember it for decades to come."[58] Under the rule of Vladimir Lenin, in the first six years of state-controlled religion it has been estimated that 28 Russian Orthodox bishops and approximately 1,200 priests were murdered by the Bolsheviks.[59] As Soviet governmental domination continued, most of the 54,000 Russian Orthodox churches operating in 1914 were either destroyed, shut down, or turned into other operations for the "good of the people." This tragic state of affairs saw no improvement after Lenin, with the introduction of Josef Stalin.

Although *glasnost* has made it possible to more clearly examine the turmoil both past and present in the USSR, it is still impossible to fully realize the extent of Soviet tyranny under Stalin. Persecution of religious believers, their persons, doctrine, and institutions was widespread and so many people died in "political" murders or for reasons such as famine that no factual data can be obtained indicating exactly how many died for their faith. Simply to be a priest during Stalin's regime was reason for an automatic prison sentence, which in Russian prisons of the time was tantamount to issuing a death sentence.

Yet despite the incredible atrocities perpetrated by Josef Stalin, there is one act of violence that stands above all the rest. Stalin systematically set about destroying every church in the Soviet Union. Those he did not destroy, he stripped of their holy trappings, putting them to some utilitarian purpose often using them as storehouses.[60] This act of Stalin's angered church goers beyond any other, and is one which Soviet Christians are not likely to forgive. The church acted as a social focal point for many rural women, who under communism had no other social outlet. Even people who were not proclaimed Christians were outraged at this sacrilege, and talked and wrote about it as often as possible under the circumstances. One Soviet writer, Alexandre Solzhenitsyn, wrote the following piece before he openly declared his faith; the words are representative of all of Russia:

> When you travel the by-roads of Central Russia you begin to understand the secret of the pacifying Russian countryside. It is in the churches. They trip up the slopes, ascend the high hills, come down to the broad rivers, like princesses in white and red, they lift their bell-towers—graceful, shapely, variegated—high over mundane timber and thatch, they nod to each other from afar, from villages that are cut off and invisible to each other they soar to the same heaven. And wherever you wander in the fields or meadows, however far from habitation, you are never alone: from over the hayricks, the wall of trees, and even the curve of the earth's surface, the head of some bell-tower will beckon you from Borki Lovetskiye, Lyubichi or Gavrilovskoye.
>
> But when you reach the village you find that not the living, but the dead greeted you from afar. The crosses were knocked off the roof or twisted out of place long ago. The dome has been stripped and there are gaping holes between its rusty ribs. Weeds grow on the roofs and in the cracks of the walls. Usually the graveyard has been neglected, its crosses

flattened and the graves churned up. Over the
years rain has penetrated to the murals over
the altar and obscene inscriptions are scrawled
over them.

In the porch there are barrels of lubricating oil
and a tractor is turning in towards them, or a
lorry has backed into the church doorway to
pick up some sacks. One church reverberates
to the shudder of lathes, another is locked and
silent. In others various groups and clubs are
meeting: 'Aim at high milk yields!' 'A poem on
peace.' 'A heroic deed.'

People were always selfish and often unkind,
but the evening chimes would ring out,
floating over villages, fields and woods,
reminding people to abandon the trivial
concerns of this world and give time and
thought to eternity...our forefathers put all that
was finest in themselves, all their
understanding of life into these stones, into
these bell-towers. 'Ram it in, Vitka,' 'give it a
bash,' 'don't be afraid!' 'Film show at six,'
'dancing at eight!'[61]

Stalin tried to redeem himself in the 1940s, after the outbreak
of the Second World War. At the beginning of the war there were
still a few hundred churches in operation in the Soviet Union
and thousands of clandestine worship services. Stalin, in a
desperate attempt to garner more support for the war effort,
convinced the remnants of the Russian Orthodox Church to
collaborate with him and support the war, and in return for such
support, gave promise of reward. He promised restoration of a
few thousand Soviet churches, to be restored over a period of

many years, while at the same time, other churches in the satellite states of Russia could also be used for worship. Thus, it was all the more catastrophic when Kruschev stepped into power, and recommenced the destruction of the Russian Orthodoxy.[62]

The year was 1959, and many Soviet Christians felt that they were on the way to complete recognition and full worship privileges when Kruschev's persecution of religion began. Stalin was denounced at the Twentieth Party Congress in 1956, and the beginning of Krushchev's rule seemed to promise a more liberal church arena. Events went in a different direction, however, as ideologues within the Kremlin, dismayed at Krushchev's liberal policies, pressured the premier into a demonstration of his loyalty to communism. Unfortunately, the way Krushchev chose to display his fealty was through attacking the most defenseless group, the church. Krushchev began claiming that the Soviet Union was finally on the true path to complete communism, and under this Marxist ideal, there would be no place for religion. Believers were savagely rooted out and imprisoned, "accidentally" assassinated, or had their reputations so undermined through political subterfuge as to be utterly shunned in Russian society.[63]

Although voices were initially silent, it was not long before certain stalwart Christians began to protest this new state of affairs, and gather together to begin openly taking a stand against the policy of the state. The Baptists of Russia and the Ukraine were the first to shout their feelings, but were soon followed by an ever-growing, though still careful, legion of

Christians of other sects. There was one man, however, who embodied the protests, and set an example that drew many isolated protesters towards an organized common goal. Father (Fr.) Gleb Yakunin, ordained as a Russian Orthodox priest in 1962, began to collect tales of atrocities being perpetrated in various regions across the country, and also began quietly spreading these tales among the clergy and concerned Christian individuals both in Russia and among Westerners visiting the USSR.[64]

Fr. Gleb enlisted one other great Soviet Christian protester, Fr. Nikolai Szolsty, and the two men took a bold stand against what was happening. Together, these men wrote two letters, one to the Soviet government, requesting justice, and the other to the Patriarch of the Eastern Orthodox Church in Istanbul begging for assistance. This was the first direct confrontational stance taken by any Soviet in any field, and nothing really came of it in the sense of actual changes.[65] However, the impact of the letters on dissident ideology in the Soviet Union cannot be denied. This is one clear example of the prominent role Christianity and its believers have played in the current downfall of the communist resistance to organized religion.

The two men were suspended from their parishes, and placed under an injunction of silence. Fr. Gleb was subjected to ten years of enforced silence and during this time the Soviet Union saw the rise to power of a new premier, Leonoid Brezhnev. Similar to the beginning of Krushchev's rule, the early years of Brezhnev's reign were full of promise, but these hopes soon evaporated, leaving the Christians more discouraged than ever. Mr. Gorbachev has referred to this period in Soviet history as the period of "stagnation" (*zastoi*).[66] Outright persecution of the churches did subside, but subtle ways of keeping the church from gaining any ground were employed by the administrative arm of the Soviet government. Churches were unable to register within their own communities, and buildings were condemned on the slightest pretext. It was during this time that Fr. Gleb once again raised his magnificent voice in protest.

Fr. Gleb took a yet bolder stance in this fray, calling for all true believers to deliberately create illegal parishes, and continue to worship. If the state would not allow a church to register, Fr. Gleb urged that the church set up its own house of prayer, in defiance of the Moscow Patriarchate, which was in the control of the government. At the time this notion seemed preposterous, but later proved to have been justified. From the standpoint of the government, this type of criticism and outright defiance could not be tolerated, and the authorities arrested Fr. Gleb on November 1, 1979. Ten months later Fr. Gleb was sentenced to ten years, five in labor camp and five in exile. This only added to his symbolism, however, and the creation of his martyrdom for the persecuted Christians, who carried on his ideas until Fr. Gleb's early release in 1987.[67]

Even though Josef Stalin's reign of terror is the most publicized, one must realize that Krushchev was at least as deadly in the demise of the Soviet Church. "Incredible as it may seem, there were three times as many churches on the day of Stalin's death as when Gorbachev came to power in 1985. This is due solely to Krushchev's destruction of the churches, not to the mass abandonment of the faith which propagandists claimed."[68]

Mikhail Gorbachev was elected on March 11, 1985, three years after the death of Brezhnev, and was immediately looked to for inspirational leadership. Between Brezhnev and Gorbachev were two miserable leaders, Yuri Andropov, who was simply too old and tired, followed by Chernenko, a public embarrassment. It was into this mess that Mr. Gorbachev walked, with ideals that he immediately proceeded to put into practice. "Events such as his ascension to power in March 1985 and the Orthodox Millenium three years later will surely go down in history as key factors in the turning of the tide for religious liberty."[69]

The man who became leader of the USSR in 1985 is a complex man, and not the least of his complexities is his deep religiosity, which he seems to have concealed during his rise to power. One can only guess at his reasons for doing so; the pessimist or cynic may say that Gorbachev simply dumped his religious background when it became inconvenient and wrapped the religious cloak around himself when it became politically expedient to present himself as a Christian. Such an idea of Gorbachev does have some clear facts which would seem to back it up. On November 28, 1986, Gorbachev was quoted calling for "a determined and pitiless combat against religious manifestations," directing this statement against the Muslim-dominated Uzbekistan area.[70]

The optimist may say that Gorbachev tried to work within the power structure and so presented no part of himself that would deny him access to that structure. Certainly this idea has as many facts supporting it as the does the pessimist. Excerpts from later reports by the Foreign Broadcast Information Service portray what seems to be a different man entirely: "President Mikhail Gorbachev met Patriarch of Moscow and all Russia Aleksey II in the Kremlin today. Gorbachev and Aleksey stressed the importance of public accord in resolving current difficulties and promoting moral values."[71] In either case, there is no denying that some background study of the man reveals that religion must have had some impact on Gorbachev at an early age.

Mr. Gorbachev was born in 1931 in a remote Stavropol Region, in the south of Russia. He was born Mikhail Sergeyevich Gorbachev, and was happy to have even a name to cling to. Approximately 30,000 people died of famine in his own region during the 1930s.[72] At the age of eleven, his world was further influenced by the hostile Nazi army which occupied his village. It was probably this event that influenced his later policy of non-intervention which resulted in the destruction of the Berlin Wall. Of course many other factors played in this event, but there is little doubt that Gorbachev 'actively non-participated' in the events leading up to and the actual fall of the Wall in 1989, and his deep-seated emotions regarding a near-fascist Germany certainly impacted his policies during this time.

Gorbachev's grandmother was a Christian, and Mikhail was baptized as a child. This woman probably attempted to teach some of her ideology to Gorbachev, but it is difficult to gauge how much impact this had, or how Gorbachev's early Christian influences withstood elementary school, secondary school and finally Moscow University. While pursuing his law degree at Moscow University, Gorbachev was required to take a course in "scientific atheism."[73]

He met and married one of his fellow students, Raisa, while completing his degree, and began climbing the party ladder, and his career in politics was launched. It was clear from the very beginning of Gorbachev's reign that policies would be changing. One of Gorbachev's first acts as premier was an attempt to abolish alcohol from the Kremlin functions, due to its obviously debilitating influence on the policy makers. Although this attempt failed, it is the first example of Gorbachev's steps in shaking the established order.[74] This first show of Gorbachev's ideas was quickly followed by the release of some prominent political prisoners, particularly Anatoli Scharansky. "He was one of the outstanding Soviet human rights activists...one of the world's best known political detainees."[75]

Another released prisoner that captured the attention of the world was the unconditional release of Irina Ratushinskaya, a young poet. She had been found guilty of writing poetry that referred to Christ in a political nature, with dissident political undertones, and sentenced in 1983, at the age of 28, to seven years in a labor camp and five years in exile. Since her release came directly after the incident at Chernobyl, many critics believed that this was merely an attempt by Gorbachev to win popular support in the world to offset the disaster of Chernobyl's nuclear reactor. Mr. Gorbachev disproved these cynics however, when two months later he ordered the release of

Andrei Sakharov, the Soviet Union's best known democratic reformer.

Mr. Gorbachev continued to show his efforts at change in a variety of ways, not just the release of popular prisoners, including creating political committees which would have far reaching impact. His human rights committee, known as the "Public Commission for Humanitarian Questions and Human Rights," a direct response to worldwide criticism of human rights under the Soviet regime, is one such political force set in motion by Gorbachev.

More importantly, however, Gorbachev seemed to be granting that religion plays a large role in the world, and accordingly, he continued to meet with church leaders on almost every one of his travels. He visited Westminster Abbey, had a private meeting with the Archbishop of Canterbury, and on December 1, 1989, Mr. Gorbachev met with the Pope at the Vatican. Beginning as early as May of 1988, Gorbachev began encouraging the growth of religion in Russia, as his historic meeting with church leaders demonstrates.

Mikhail Gorbachev met with Patriarch Pimen of Moscow and All Russia and members of the Holy Synod of the Russian Orthodox Church for an hour and a half on April 29. Ninety minutes may not seem like much time. But the significance of this meeting cannot be measured by the time allotted it. Even some of the good ideas it generated...pale when compared with the significance for our society of that dialogue in the Kremlin.[76]

He did not limit himself to meeting with Russian church officials within the USSR, however; recognizing the universality of religion's role for people, Gorbachev received the Vatican Secretary of State in Moscow. Cardinal Agostino Casaroli was invited to Moscow by the Russian Orthodox Church to attend festivities marking 1,000 years of Christianity in Russia. Talks between Gorbachev and the Cardinal resulted in a statement that a meeting with the Pope in Russia would be in the near future.[77]

Eventually Gorbachev's evidenced respect for religion gave rise to a request by the Dalai Lama for a meeting. Unfortunately, this meeting did not take place because of intense political relationships with China, but the significance is not lost. The spiritual leader of a nation displaced by communism seeking to meet with the head of the Soviet Union certainly points to the role of religion in Gorbachev's opening of the Iron Curtain.[78] Eventually, the church, encouraged by Gorbachev, began to take an increasingly active role in the political events of the time. On August 20, 1991, "The head of the Russian Orthodox Church expressed hope that 'the peoples of our country will be able to put their house in accordance with free elections and the universally accepted standards of morality and law.'"[79] It should not be overlooked that the Patriarch at this time, Aleksey II, was the first Patriarch to be elected "free of manipulation by the atheistic regime."[80] In fact, further demonstrating the political results of religion, the man elected was not Russian. Aleksay was in fact an Estonian of German descent, and his election by the religious authorities clearly had dramatic impact on the way Russian believers though about the rest of the world. It is clear that Mr. Gorbachev hearkened back to an earlier day, in which religion played a vital role in the maintenance of daily life, without being politically dominated. Although he met opposition at every turn, he handled each hurdle well, ever-expanding the influence of religion in the tumultuous events of his reign.

The course set by Gorbachev was followed closely by Russian President Boris Yeltsin. It was obvious that Yeltsin too realized the importance of religion in the downfall of the communist regime, and in maintaining a healthy society. On November 22, 1991, Yeltsin signed a decree "allowing the Patriarch to use some of the Kremlin churches" in accordance with all Christian activities.[81] Yeltsin continued to increase the outward role of religion, seeking unity among Muslims and other faiths, returning religious property to the Russian Orthodoxy, and on December 6, 1991, Yeltsin appealed to the heads of churches and all believers to be the leaders in making peace during the difficult time of reforms.[82]

Historically, the territory of the Soviet Union has been under autocratic rule for many centuries. Now, in the first years of *glasnost*, the world is witnessing difficulty as the responsibility for governing moves slowly away from the bureaucracy to the people. Religion, with its emphasis on the importance of the individual and the individual's right to seek meaning in existence, may provide, along with Mr. Gorbachev's early policy changes, the needed structural bridge to true democracy in the Soviet Union. Marxism is dying, fatally wounded by its own failures and contradictions. Where do these contradictions originate? They begin with the attempt by the Soviet Union to suppress religion, one of mankind's most treasured possessions.

Of course, it is also possible that religion will turn out to have rather more dramatic effects, quite possibly negative. In writing about Russia's search for a post-communist identity in a post-modern world, Mikhail Sergeev paints a plausible picture of "neo-conservative" post-modernism resulting in religious nationalism of extreme fundamentalism.[83] However, this further demonstrates the power of religion in reshaping a society during times of revolution and reform. Even if the end result can be portrayed somewhat negatively, as the term fundamentalism has come to be understood, the force of the social phenomenon of religion cannot be ignored.

Although it is difficult to predict, it seems likely that if the three remaining communist societies undergo revolution, religion will play some role. In all three of the surviving communist states, religion has historically been an integral part of the society, and may come to the forefront in any attempts to overthrow the governments. China has two distinct religious traditions which still have enormous impact on the people. Buddhism, and to an even greater extent, Taoism, have tremendous respect for essential truths of the universe which supersede mankind's rules entirely. Taoism has at its core a basic faith of right and wrong, and absolute rule by man is wrong, unless it is acknowledged that the ruling power is given by a god. In Buddhism, although there is no belief in an absolute god, there is absolute belief in man, and in particular, man as an unenlightened being, therefore not deserving of any sort of power, much less that used by communist governments. It is this form of Buddhism, called Mahayana Buddhism, that prevails in North Korea even today, and may result in the eventual disillusionment with the regime that culminates in revolution. In Cuba, the elements of Catholicism that have engulfed South America in a theological frenzy are present and strong. The very name of this evolution of Catholicism, "liberation theology," speaks for itself. Although the theology's initial expounders were Marxian-influenced intellectuals, the theology has since come to mean a glorification of the poor, and a quest for a "super human"—one whose consciousness has been raised through religious experience. Such an experience cannot take place under suppression, and this may indeed provide a seed of extreme discontent that grows rather suddenly in Cuba. Much of the populist millennialism spread by Castro sprang from Christian archetypes, which cannot be entirely remade, and may one day come back to haunt Castro.

The importance of religion in the foundations of a country and in its gradual shift to revolutionary activity cannot be overlooked. When studying the dynamics of revolution from the perspective of social history, one must carefully look at the people's faith, because it is that faith which will help shape their faith in themselves and the new government they hope to create.

Religion and Terrorism

Violence and the Sacred

in the 21st Century

NOTE: Portions of this article first appeared in *Terrorism: A Global Survey*, a special report by Jane's Information Group. ISBN: 0 7106 1662 7.

INTRODUCTION

In our world of rapidly changing borders, cross-cultural business dealings and globalization, security issues between nation-states remain a priority, but terrorism is perhaps the first truly global security concern. Acts of violence by terrorists are difficult by their very nature to track, predict and counter, and as events of the past few years have shown, terrorism can strike literally anywhere. At least with political (i.e., secular) terrorism, the global community may foresee the conflict and realize that a political action of violence may be forthcoming (for example, in response to new legislation, perhaps a change in the legal status of a group defined by the nation-state in which they reside). In the case of religious terrorism, the possibility of a small group of fanatics perceiving a theological mandate to commit violence is far more difficult to predict and to prepare for and counter. In religiously-motivated violence, because the mandate is from the highest power, the perpetrators are in their own minds immune from the normal laws governing us, and can commit acts of atrocity that would normally be reviled. Yet we must find a way of approaching religious terrorism systematically, in order to construct a means of confronting it as a global society, and develop strategies to combat it. In essence, we must explore the attempts of an emerging global society to account for the phenomena of disparate faiths and value-systems as technology brings those disparate cultures into ever closer proximity, with often explosive results.

As the 21st century marches forward into an increasingly religiously-charged society of violence, beginning with the attacks on the World Trade Towers on September 11, 2001, and continuing through the Iraq War, we need to ask ourselves some questions about religious terrorism, in order to prepare for the increase in acts of religious terrorism around the world. From a security standpoint, we have several starting points for a discussion about religious terrorism: What is the nature of religious terrorism? What is the current status of the world with regards to religious terrorism? How is religious terrorism changing at the end of the millennium? Who should be concerning themselves with religious terrorism? What, if any, is the role of the military and other governmental structures in combating religious terrorism?

WHAT IS THE NATURE OF RELIGIOUS TERRORISM?
Religious terrorism is usually defined as acts of violence perpetrated by members of a certain religious belief structure, against those whose different belief structures are in conflict with

the terrorists. (This definition serves as a good starting point, but we shall see that is not as hard and fast a definition as it once was.) Such conflicts are often deemed intractable by many, causing the interested parties (such as the United Nations, conflict resolution theorists, negotiators and other NGOs) to focus on peripheral issues, stating that religious terrorism is the hardest form of terrorism to approach. In fact, nothing could be further than the truth. Although humans vary immensely in their beliefs, the similarity is that almost everyone has beliefs, and different groups have gone through similar processes to arrive at their current belief structure; given time and opportunity, one can apply similar processes to arrive at an understanding of different religions and of religious terrorism. Such an approach must begin with the question of why violence is the usual recourse of these fanatics.

If we take as a given that violence is inherent in life on this earth and has been since throughout human history, then we must realize that organized religions, mythologies and belief structures must account for violence. Although arguments can certainly be made on both sides of the question, "Is violence inherent in humanity?" it cannot be denied that violent acts occur in nature, and must be dealt with by humanity as witnesses to creation. As people are confronted with violence, they must find a way of coping with violence and its chaotic effects, and ways of restoring order to the world. French historian René Girard has discussed the idea that sacrifice restores order to society, and it is here that we must look for the means by which religious organizations justify acts of terrorism.

Religion imposes order on violence, yet ironically it frequently uses violence to restore order in "extreme" situations. It is important to realize that the acts of terrorism in recent years are not random, nor are they temporary. The fact is that these events are reactions against a perceived disorder, and as such are permanent fixtures in the cycle of religious belief. It is unlikely that there will be a sudden downturn in the number of religious terrorist attacks.

To understand religious terrorism, we must seek to make explicit the dynamics involved in religiously-justified violence, in order to clarify and categorize theoretical issues which will then lead to a greater understanding of religious terrorism, and a greater awareness of the characteristics of religious terrorists. At the same time, we must reach a point where we move beyond irrational fears, and cease equating certain groups with terrorism as the media has often done by pounding such rhetorical formulas as "Islam=Jihad=Muslim Terrorism" into the popular consciousness. There is no doubt that acts of terrorism are perpetrated by Muslims, but it is not an ingrained aspect of the Islamic faith (at least not any more than the precepts of violence which are embedded in Christianity) and acts of violence easily classified as terrorism are perpetrated by people with various religious affiliations including Hindu, Sikh, Buddhist, Christian, and Aum Shinrikyo (the cult which unleashed chemical weaponry on subway commuters in Japan).

Most acts of terrorism are considered political in nature, but many are religiously based, and even those acts which are explicitly political often have religious underpinnings. We can see a difference between "pure political" terrorism and "pure religious" terrorism by understanding the different targets for each. Politically motivated acts of terrorism are usually directed towards a clear target, either an entity or structure representing the state, with the goal being an act of destruction which will cause the state to respond in a manner conducive to the internal goals of the terrorists. In such cases the use of terrorism is often a coercive move, although not always. In an act of religious terrorism, the target is more loosely defined—it is simply some representation of those who disagree with the terrorists' belief system. This began changing in the final years of the last millennium, however; targets simultaneously became more diffuse on a smaller scale and more targeted on a larger scale. The predictability of possible targets for religious terrorists began decreasing as they unleashed violence on seemingly randomly chosen victims, such as the subway commuters in Japan's Sarin attack of 1995, or the fact that Al-Qaeda's goals are simply to "strike at the West," meaning essentially all people and places are targets at all times. The goal of acts of religious terrorism is also less clear. Often the goal is simply to lash out at the "unbelievers" in a way which is harmful enough to be noticed throughout the community. It is rare that such acts of "pure" terrorism occur, however, which is what makes religion and terrorism such a crucial topic in today's global society. Despite the acute need for broad discussion and investigation of religious terrorism, the discourse has yet to reach useful levels. We must create and place this discourse in the context of an emerging global society reacting to the telecommunications revolution both by becoming smaller and more integrated, but also by social/cultural boundaries coming into closer proximity, and chafing, in what Dr. Samuel Huntington has called "the clash of civilizations" in his book of the same name.

What Is the Current Status of the World with Regards to Religious Terrorism?

We have myriad examples of religious terrorism in the recent past—both out-of-context single events and ongoing situations; the original bombing of the World Trade Center and its final reckoning on 9/11, the explosion in Oklahoma City, and ongoing conflicts in Ireland, Sudan and Bosnia are just a few of the most widely discussed. Here we see that acts of terrorism are often both political and religiously motivated. The explosion in Oklahoma City is a prime example of a terrorist event with primarily political motivation, but with roots in religious doctrine, both explicit and surmised. We have events of violence which are as yet completely unexplained—at least in public at the time of this article—such as the Olympic pipe bomb in Atlanta in 1996, and the explosion of TWA flight 800, in which terrorism is still being discussed as a possible reason, despite final NTSB findings as to the cause of the accident. This raises a disturbing question: Have acts of religious terrorism become so diffuse, so random in the recent past that we cannot successfully hypothesize as to their motivation and probable perpetrators after the fact, much less before? If so, the security forces of the world are in a difficult situation. Even in situations where the perpetrator is caught, as in the Oklahoma bombing, we are at a loss to explain how we might have adequately been prepared for such an event, even given the widespread discussion of politically motivated splinter groups.

The Oklahoma case is particularly illuminating to an examination of the role of religion and terrorism as it was immediately and incorrectly viewed as a religious terrorist attack by the most likely culprits: Muslims. It is interesting to reflect here that when terrorist events of almost unbelievable atrocity occur, victims and witnesses are most likely to suspect religious motivation; the worldwide fear of religious fanaticism is universal in its response to acts of violence, and lack of understanding of other religions. Anyone listening to the news that day would have heard The White House declaiming the event as an "an attack against America and the way we live!" Followed quickly by the media's loud pronouncements about the FBI conducting a "search for men of Middle Eastern origin" and constant references to the Muslims in court in New York, it takes little imagination to see how even a non-radicalized Muslim would begin to decry the constant fear-mongering towards the Islamic community. President Clinton, along with a professor of terrorism at Oklahoma University and other media personalities ramped up the rhetoric, and pointed a finger of blame towards unknown Islamic radical terrorists, and average citizens began to react.

The effect on the populace of such rhetoric cannot be dismissed, as it furthers religiously motivated distrust and enters into the cycle of culture-clash that perpetuates radical responses to differences in religious belief. When journalist Mark Steyn was visiting Oklahoma City soon after the bomb he heard a woman working at a restaurant say that she swore if an "Islam person" were to come in she would refuse to serve him. On the internet, discussion groups and websites sprung up to track Muslim actions and suspected Islamic groups, and the electronic rooms of the world of cyberspace were ringing with hate-email.

An American self-styled patriot ultimately was found to be responsible, but the implications of the early statements and whispers in America underscore the fact that "Islam" still strikes a chord of fear in many Western hearts and minds. Clearly there is a need for greater understanding of Islamic ideals in many areas. More importantly, this event and its surrounding media coverage explicate causes of escalating religious terrorism; misunderstanding and fear fanned by an increasingly electronic media-interconnected world which responds to media coverage so rapidly that it creates an immediate complex discourse often based on false premises.

The media refuses to learn its lesson though, and now broadcasts all sorts of opinions on why suspect Timothy McVeigh parked his fertilizer bomb-laden truck outside the Oklahoma City Federal Building. Most often discussed is the date of April 19 which is extrapolated to attribute the bombing to a reaction to the situation in Waco, Texas, when the Branch Davidians eventually set their compound and themselves aflame rather than submit to federal authorities. The implication is that McVeigh was objecting to what he perceived as restrictions of freedom of religion, as well as overzealous federal power, but these are mere speculations, possibly as fatuous as those made about Islamic suspects earlier in the year.

How Did Religious Terrorism Begin Changing at the End of the Last Millennium?

The changing of the millennium was felt as a threatening rather than encouraging event by many people, as the discourse surrounding the event had somber undertones. This helped shape a global response of fear about random acts of violence, a fear which became increasingly obvious as splinter groups began to voice concerns about the end of the millennium and those voices penetrated mainstream society. Discussion of millenarian mythology passed beyond the academic and into the mainstream; even in popular culture, on television, one of the most talked about shows of the 1996/97 season was Millennium, a gothic US show about a group of men and women dedicated to fighting the random acts of violence perpetrated by society's darker, usually fanatically religious side in reaction to the approaching millennium. Those people were terrorists in the ultimate sense of the word as it used in popular parlance: striking out with violent acts in seemingly random events, inculcating terror in those people affected. Yet this is not the actual definition of terrorism, which in fact implies a systematic use of terror, planned events of violence for a specific purpose, although the target of the violence may in fact be random.

Recent religious terrorism has changed the nature of violence as it embraces less conservative weaponry. Terrorism has long brought to mind visions of bombs and hostage-taking, and although these continue to be weapons of the religious terrorist, new forms of violence are being unleashed on unsuspecting citizens. Perhaps the most shocking of these new terrorist weapons at the end of the millennium was used in Japan, by an obscure cult led by blind religious recluse Shoko Asahara. The group Aum Shinrikyo was founded in 1987 by Asahara, and rapidly began stockpiling dangerous chemicals. Eventually the cult combined these chemicals in so-called binary bombs, releasing the deadly nerve gas Sarin into the subway. Justification for the act was in the groups' doomsday ideas. As the year 2000 began to approach, the belief was that the world would end in cataclysmic events, after which adherents to the faith would find themselves in paradise. A millennial group such as Aum Shinrikyo feels the need to become an active player in these events by hastening the demise of the unbelievers. The use of chemical and biological weapons began increasing in groups like Aum Shinrikyo, as they began to prepare for the end of the millennium. According to the judge who presided over the case of the bomb at the World Trade Center, the bomb itself was also packed with cyanide to poison the surrounding area; the plan failed because the cyanide burned during the explosion. US-based white supremacist groups also began stockpiling cyanide in the early 1980s, and in 1986, members of Bhagwan Shree Rajneesh's cult deliberately caused a salmonella epidemic. These types of weapons are the latest in attacking people directly, but other kinds of attacks are also on the rise: the events of 9/11 showed the world that planes with no bombs or chemicals aboard could still serve as weapons of enormous destruction. Information warfare, which hadn't even been considered much of a threat as recently as ten years ago, is now taking on prominence in security discussions.

One of the wonders of the age is the internet, and the global society being created through the interlinking of computer systems worldwide, stimulating the flow of information. As this system makes inroads into all levels of human interaction, the potential for a whole new kind of terrorist attack emerges: information warfare. The incidents of "hacking" are on the rise worldwide, and often the perpetrator is invisible. There is no doubt that religious groups are computer-savvy, and are using the internet as a meeting and planning place, as well as a place to broadcast their beliefs and calls for action. There is ample reason to believe that they will (if they are not already doing so) use the internet and related technologies to engage in acts of destruction to further their goals. The apocalyptic aspects of some of these groups are showing up in manifestos they are publishing electronically, giving a clear indication that they will take action in the near future.

One final horror also needs to be addressed in discussing the changing face of religious terrorism. Since the downfall of the Soviet Union, a remarkable amount of dangerous radioactive material such as is used in nuclear warheads is "missing." The possibility of this material falling into the hand of a terrorist organization is not one to be ignored. It is known that Saddam Hussein had scientists working on giving Iraq nuclear capability, and although it seems that he never succeeded in actually building a WMD (weapon of mass destruction), given the state support of a variety of terrorist groups in the Middle East, there is the chance of a nuclear weapon being deliberately used in an act of religious terrorism. The normal restraints against using nuclear weaponry which have held its use in check by nation-states are not recognized by religious terrorists, and for that reason this is perhaps the greatest concern of any security-minded global organization.

Another aspect of religious terrorism which is changing most noticeably is locale, particularly in the United States. Until relatively recently, religious terrorist attacks have been primarily events which occurred outside the nation's boundaries. It was something that happened in troubled areas such as Northern Ireland or in Israel. Most of the events of terrorism in Europe can be deemed political actions rather than religiously based; if religious terrorism did happen in someplace like Madrid or Paris, it was because the terrorists were making a point of striking against another government. But in recent years the spate of events inside the United States' borders has increased, and perhaps most disheartening for Americans is the fact that many of these events are perpetrated by other Americans. The 9/11 planes striking the World Trade Center of course stands out as the largest of these events, but abortion center bombings, assassination of abortion doctors, and the fact that militia movements are gaining adherents contributes to a feeling of impending doom. Aum Shinrikyo and other cults also have members in the United States, and the goals of these groups and their members' willingness to carry out bizarre attacks are suspect at best.

What is particularly interesting is the larger role that apocalyptic dialogue is having on the internal goals of these groups. Biblical ideals of Armageddon are becoming the central force in the decision making processes of many terrorist groups, and there is an increasing likelihood of previously relatively quiescent groups suddenly turning violent. Any movement which anticipates imminent, total supernatural salvation view themselves as having a divine imperative to have a participatory role in the "last days." Given the impetus to hasten salvation, these groups may feel that their particular role is to assist in "judgment day," thus the predilection towards destruction. As judgment against unbelievers would clearly result in their chance at salvation being slim at best, the death resulting from a religiously motivated act of violence is not one which is inherently evil in the eyes of the deity of the terrorist group.

WHO SHOULD BE CONCERNING THEMSELVES WITH RELIGIOUS TERRORISM?

For years a distinction has been drawn between foreign and domestic terrorism, and that division has resulted in a weak response to religious terrorism which crosses boundaries of all sorts, political, geographical and cultural. Domestic terrorism is assigned to a nation-state's internal peace-keeping forces, often with the result that any intelligence gathering on the organization's ties to groups outside the state is somewhat lacking, and thus a response is incomplete. Foreign religious terrorism is almost deemed to be "understandable," and perhaps unavoidable in Huntington's "clash of civilizations." If any attempt to respond is made on a global basis, it is usually to reframe the event as political, and then pass it on to the military. This has the result of legitimizing the terrorist event, as the media picks up the story and it becomes a mini-war, played out on the television screens of the masses.

Religious terrorism can be bound up in political dissent, but the global aspects of religious terrorism outside of nation-state disputes calls for a global response outside of any nation-state's military, and outside of the United Nation' peace-keeping forces. In 1986, then ambassador Benjamin Netanyahu wrote of his theories about winning the war against terrorism in his book *Terrorism: How the West Can Win*, missing the crucial point that the West cannot win this war, although it can contribute a great deal to a global community response to religious terrorism. The title seems regrettable from a cultural standpoint, seeming to assert that the West stands together and disregards the East, implying that the East is either not involved (after the Aum Shinrikyo event, this would be a particularly disturbing standpoint), that the East is the origin of terrorism (after the Oklahoma bombing, also a vapid viewpoint), or perhaps worse, that the West does not need the East to successfully combat religious terrorism. Netanyahu also strives to make clear the fact that underlying all responses to terrorism—political, economic, military—there must be a moral basis upon which to build a successful strategy to combat terrorism. It would seem that for a moral response to religious terrorism to have any validity in the global community, such a basis must be worked towards by the West and the East, giving at least a moderately universal sense to the foundation of a global war against terrorism. Given Netanyahu's current position in the political arena, it will be interesting to observe his actions and see whether they dovetail with earlier assertions.

Regardless, the point must be made here that Netanyahu and other contributors to his book accept as a given that everyone in the West can reach a moral understanding of universal truths. However, it can probably already be agreed that acts of terrorism are are found to be abhorrent by the majority, and this is a strong enough basis upon which to form a front against religious terrorism. To entangle counter-terrorism in discussions of morality would merely prolong the time to reach a useful response. So we are left with the attempt to frame an international response to religious terrorism, with the obvious understanding that the response must be universal in its agreement that religious terrorism is inherently counter-productive to the global community, and that a response must be unified at the political, military and economic layers of the world society. A task immense in scope, and unprecedented, but not impossible.

Should an international organization be formed with full funding from a variety of nations? Without a doubt, the answer must be an emphatic "yes." Should such an organization be organized under the United Nations as many have suggested? The answer here must be just as emphatic, but must be "no." Regrettably, the UN has lost a great deal of credibility, and its top-heavy bureaucracy and entangling web of missions would be at best detrimental to a focused global response to religious terrorism. As Netanyahu pointed out, it is doubtful that many would disagree with Churchill's dictum that protection of its citizens is a government's first obligation. We must now extrapolate Churchill's idea and state that a civilized world's first obligation is to protect its law-abiding citizens against the acts of those who would endanger those citizens, hindering the creation of a just, participatory and sustainable society in which sustainability is at least partially measured by stable, relatively permanent peace.

It is possible that even the existence of an organization proven to be taking into account the phenomena of disparate faiths as part and parcel of an ongoing, determined struggle against terrorism would be useful in curbing the need of religious terrorists to make themselves heard through violence, as long as it was clear what the response to that violence would be. More importantly, it must be understood that the response would not vary from event to event depending on locale, victims, and supposed motivation. Herein lies perhaps the most critical aspect of any organization devoted to fighting terrorism: the response must be pre-determined, rugged, and it must be known to the terrorists of the world. The form of the response itself can of course be argued, but it would behoove the founders of such an organization to examine historical evidence, leading them to the realization that there are several keys to a relatively successful response to terrorism.

Netanyahu and others have pointed out that simple non-capitulation is the most important factor in dissuading terrorists, as terrorism sets out to make a point, after which demands will be made. This is not always the case in religiously motivated terrorism. An act of religious terrorism may simply be a "judgment," as was discussed earlier. So refusal to deal with the terrorists is a moot point in many cases of "pure" religious terrorism, where no "deal" is envisioned. In fact, as has been discussed earlier, the diffusion of religious terrorism would indicate that the perpetrator may not even be known. We are left with the one relatively proven successful response to terrorism being somewhat useless with regards to religious terrorism. However, it does point to the immense need for intelligence-gathering on the part of all nations, and the immediate sharing of that intelligence. This in turn requires a forum, and necessitates the need for a single-minded organization to be formed. Once intelligence is placed in the hands of an international organization with some power to act internationally, the knowledge can be applied in a variety of counter-measures, including infiltration prior to an act of terrorism, or at the very least informed military response. Details of this remain to be studied and formulated, but to state the obvious, knowledge often is power.

CONCLUSIONS

It seems clear that the time for thorough investigation and discussion of religious terrorism has never been more clearly defined. If the world is to move into the 21st century safely, a discourse surrounding religious terrorism must become a part of the global consciousness. With the political paradigmatic shift from "realism" (state independence) to "pluralism" (inter-dependence) the world is faced with the necessity of creating a global ethic, upon which the members of a forthcoming "global village" can base decisions, without compromising the unique identity of any particular tradition. Any world order must take into account the questions of transcendence and search for meaning beyond the mundane that arise in human nature, resulting in belief systems and conceptions of "rights." As the forces of "modernity" march inexorably forward, questions of meaning become tantamount to survival in an increasingly cross-cultural world, and the flames of symbolic violence quickly escalate into the fires of terrorism.

Symbolic religious violence is being manifested as real, physical political violence in the contemporary world, in such events as the destruction of the World Trade Center, and recent and ongoing activities of Hizbollah, Hamas, religious belief structures in opposition resulting in terrorist acts in the ongoing Jerusalem issue, the war in Bosnia, and the cluster of conflicts in Africa. We will find that as the 21st century progresses, such events will take on a deeper meaning for those groups religiously motivated to inculcate change by exercising violence. Exploration of the conjunction of religion and technology with respect to issues such as: religious resurgence; religious militancy or "fundamentalism;" new religious movements; democratization and related ideas; and the importance of these issues in the discourse surrounding both domestic and international political conflicts can only lead to better preparedness on the part of states and international organizations. The form of such global organizations remains to be constructed, but the means, the idea, and certainly the need, is present.

Endnotes

[1] Hugo Adam Bedau, "International Human Rights," in Tom Regan and Donald VanDeVeer, eds. *And Justice For All.* (Totowa: New Jersey, 1982), 289.

[2] Hugo Adam Bedau, "International Human Rights," in Tom Regan and Donald VanDeVeer, eds. *And Justice For All.* (Totowa: New Jersey, 1982), 291.

[3] These are the main points of Bedau's statement on the necessary elements of a theory of human rights, extrapolated from his section 'The Elements of Human Rights', in Hugo Adam Bedau, "International Human Rights", in Tom Regan and Donald VanDeVeer, eds. *And Justice For All* (Totowa: New Jersey, 1982), 289. Bedau provides this statement as a foreword to his attempt to dissect the notion of a human right in the international context down to a point where agreement can be reached. He fails in this, however, by concluding his essay with a statement of how nations ignore violations of human rights, without ever clarifying in his essay an initial point of agreement for nation states based on differing ideologies.

[4] J. Bryan Hehir, "Human Rights From a Theological Perspective," in *The Moral Imperatives of Human Rights: A World Survey*, ed. Kenneth W. Thompson. (Washington, DC: University Press of America, 1980), 4.

[5] Henry Rosemont puts forth his ideas of concept clusters in his essay "Why Take Rights Seriously? A Confucian Critique," in *Human Rights in the World's Religions*, Leroy Rouner, ed. (Notre Dame: University of Notre Dame Press, 1988), 167-183.

[6] J. Bryan Hehir, "Human Rights From a Theological Perspective," in *The Moral Imperatives of Human Rights: A World Survey*, ed. Kenneth W. Thompson. (Washington, DC: University Press of America, 1980), 5.

[7] Richard Harries, "Human Rights in theological perspective," in *Human Rights for the 1990s: Legal, Political and Ethical Issues*, eds. Robert Blackburn and John Taylor (London: Mansell Publishing Limited, 1991), 1.

[8] Richard Harries, "Human Rights in theological perspective," in Human Rights for the 1990s: legal, political and ethical issues, eds. Robert Blackburn and John Taylor (London: Mansell Publishing Limited, 1991), 3.

[9] J. Bryan Hehir, "Human Rights From a Theological Perspective", in The Moral Imperatives of Human Rights: A World Survey, ed. Kenneth W. Thompson. (Washington, DC: University Press of America, 1980), 5.

[10] Richard Harries, "Human Rights in theological perspective", in Human Rights for the 1990s: legal, political and ethical issues, eds. Robert Blackburn and John Taylor (London: Mansell Publishing Limited, 1991), 9.

[11] Quran, as cited by James P. Piscatori, "Human rights in Islamic Political Culture", in The Moral Imperatives of Human Rights: A World Survey, ed. Kenneth W. Thompson. (Washington, DC: University Press of America, 1980), 139.

[12] J. Bryan Hehir, "Human Rights From a Theological Perspective", in The Moral Imperatives of Human Rights: A World Survey, ed. Kenneth W. Thompson. (Washington, DC: University Press of America, 1980), 8.

[13] J. Bryan Hehir, "Human Rights From a Theological Perspective", in The Moral Imperatives of Human Rights: A World Survey, ed. Kenneth W. Thompson. (Washington, DC: University Press of America, 1980), 9.

[14] Wesley Hohfield was an American legal theorist of the early 20th century. For a brief discussion of Hohfields four types of rights, see Lawrence C. Becker, "Individual Rights", in Tom Regan and Donald VanDeVeer, eds. And Justice For All (Totowa: New Jersey, 1982), 201.

[15] John L. Esposito, *Islam: The Straight Path* (New York: Oxford University Press, 1991), 79.

[16] Majid Khadduri, *The Islamic Conception of Justice* (Baltimore: Johns Hopkins University Press, 1984), 2-3.

[17] Majid Khadduri, *The Islamic Conception of Justice* (Baltimore: Johns Hopkins University Press, 1984), 136-137.

[18] See John L. Esposito, *Islam: The Straight Path* (New York: Oxford University Press, 1991), Chapter 1, for a further discussion of the history of Muhammad and the basis of the *hadith, sunna*, and the *Qur'an*.

[19] Majid Khadduri, *The Islamic Conception of Justice* (Baltimore: Johns Hopkins University Press, 984), 135.

[20] Glenn E. Perry, "The Islamic World: Egypt and Iran," p. 102, in *Politics and Religion in the Modern World*, ed. George Moyser (London: Routledge, 1991), 97-135.

[21] Daniel Pipes, "Fundamentalist Muslims in World Politics," p. 124, in *Secularization and Fundamentalism Reconsidered*, vol. III (New York: Paragon, 1989), 123-132.

[22] Fatima Mernissi, *Islam and Democracy: Fear of the Modern World* (New York: Addison and Wesley, 1993), 25.

[23] John L. Esposito, *Islam: The Straight Path* (New York: Oxford University Press, 1991), 78-79.

[24] W. Montgomery Watt, *What is Islam?* (London: Longman Group, 1968), 124.

[25] Fatima Mernissi, *Islam and Democracy: Fear of the Modern World* (New York: Addison and Wesley, 1993), 37.

[26] John L. Esposito, *Islam: The Straight Path* (New York: Oxford University Press, 1991), 125-126.

[27] Daniel Pipes, "Fundamentalist Muslims in World Politics," p. 123-125, in *Secularization and Fundamentalism Reconsidered*, vol. III (New York: Paragon, 1989), 123-132.

[28] Robin Wright, "Islam confronts its Luther in Iran," (*The Guardian*, 2 February 1995).

[29] Abdol Karim Soroush, quoted in Robin Wright, "Islam confronts its Luther in Iran," (*The Guardian*, 2 February 1995).

[30] Abdol Karim Soroush, quoted in Robin Wright, "Islam confronts its Luther in Iran," (*The Guardian*, 2 February 1995).

[31] Friedhelm Hardy, "The Classical Religions of India," p. 39, in *The Religions of Asia*, ed. Friedhelm Hardy, (London: Routledge, 1990), 37-128.

[32] Mark Juergensmeyer, "India," in *Religion in Politics: A World Guide*, ed. Stuart Mews (Longman: London, 1989), 98-107.

[33] For a brief discussion of the *sati* of 18-year old Roop Kanwar, see Mark Juergensmeyer, "India", in *Religion in Politics: A World Guide*, ed. Stuart Mews (Longman: London, 1989), 98-107.

[34] As quoted by Gavin Flood of University of Wales, Lampeter, in a lecture.

[35] Shikha Trivedy, "The Followers of Godse," *Manushi* 79 (1994), 2.

[36] Report of the Brandt Commission, as quoted in Norman Myers, ed. *The Gaia Atlas of Planet Management* (London: Pan Books, 1985).

[37] Derek Wall, *Green History: A reader in environmental literature, philosophy and politics* (London: Routledge, 1994), 192.

[38] Mawil Izzi Deen, "Islamic environmental ethics, law, and society," in *Ethics of Environment and Development: Global Challenge, International Response*, eds. J. Ronald Engel and Joan Gibb Engel (London: Belhaven Press, 1990).

[39] Islamic scholar at University of Wales, Lampeter, and author of several articles and books regarding Islam and the environment.

[40] Ziauddin Sardar is an Islamic writer concerned with Islam and science issues, including natural and social sciences, who has written about the Islamization of knowledge with regard to scientific issues.

[41] Author of *The Encounter of Man and Nature* (London: Allen & Unwin, 1968).

[42] Syed Hassein Nasr, *The Encounter of Man and Nature* (London: Allen & Unwin, 1968), 94-5.

[43] Derek Wall, *Green History: A reader in environmental literature, philosophy and politics* (London: Routledge, 1994), 193.

[44] Mawil Izzi Deen, "Islamic environmental ethics, law, and society," in *Ethics of Environment and Development: Global Challenge, International Response*, eds. J. Ronald Engel and Joan Gibb Engel (London: Belhaven Press, 1990).

[45] Mawil Izzi Deen, "Islamic environmental ethics, law, and society," in *Ethics of Environment and Development: Global Challenge, International Response*, eds. J. Ronald Engel and Joan Gibb Engel (London: Belhaven Press, 1990).

[46] All Biblical quotations are from the *New International Version*.

[47] Mawil Izzi Deen, "Islamic environmental ethics, law, and society," in *Ethics of Environment and Development: Global Challenge, International Response*, eds. J. Ronald Engel and Joan Gibb Engel (London: Belhaven Press, 1990).

[48] Mawil Izzi Deen, "Islamic environmental ethics, law, and society," in *Ethics of Environment and Development: Global Challenge, International Response*, eds. J. Ronald Engel and Joan Gibb Engel (London: Belhaven Press, 1990).

[49] Martin Palmer, Anne Nash and Ivan Hattingh, (eds.) *Faith and Nature: Our relationship with the natural world explored through sacred literature* (London: WWF, 1987).

[50] All eight of the specific Islamic reasons for protection of the environment discussed in this paper are taken from the essay by Mawil Izzi Deen, "Islamic environmental ethics, law, and society" in *Ethics of Environment and Development: Global Challenge, International Response*, eds. J. Ronald Engel and Joan Gibb Engel (London: Belhaven Press, 1990).

[51] Mawil Izzi Deen, "Islamic environmental ethics, law, and society" in *Ethics of Environment and Development: Global Challenge, International Response*, eds. J. Ronald Engel and Joan Gibb Engel (London: Belhaven Press, 1990).

[52] Martin Palmer, Anne Nash and Ivan Hattingh (eds). *Faith and Nature: Our relationship with the world explored through sacred literature* (London: WWF, 1987).

[53] Paul Tillich, *Dynamics of Faith* (New York: Harper & Row, 1958), 1-5.

[54] Ibid., 23.

[55] Olga Kerkina, "Religious Liberty in Russia," *Upbeat* vol 4., no. 6 (1994): 19.

[56] Hackel, Sergei, "The Orthodox Churches of Eastern Europe," in *The Oxford Illustrated History of Christianity*, ed. John McManners (Oxford: Oxford University Press, 1992), 520-522.

[57] Michael Bordeaux, *Gorbachev, Glasnost & The Gospel* (London: Hodder & Stoughton, 1990), 1.

[58] Peter Reddaway, ed. & trans, *Uncensored Russia: Protest and Dissent in the Soviet Union* (Great Britain: American Heritage Press, 1972), 34.

[59] Trevor Beeson, *Discretion and Valor* (London: Keston Press, 1982), 97. Beeson's statistics are based on an emigre church source who maintained close contacts with the Soviet Union during the years immediately following the 1917 revolution.

[60] Michael Bordeaux, *Patriarch and Prophets: Persecution of the Russian Orthodox Church* (London: Mowbrays, 1975), 131-48.

[61] Ibid., 154-155.

[62] Hackel, "The Orthodox Churches of Eastern Europe," 539-541.

[63] Hill, *Puzzle of the Soviet Church*, 45-51.

[64] Bordeaux, *Gorbachev, Glasnost & The Gospel*, 7-8.

[65] Reddaway, *Protest and Dissent*, 98-104.

[66] Bordeaux, *Gorbachev, Glasnost & The Gospel* 79-81.

[67] Ibid., 104-105.

[68] Bordeaux, *Gorbachev, Glasnost & The Gospel*, 111.

[69] Ibid. 21.

[70] Foreign Broadcast Information Service, "Gorbachev Calls for Crackdown Against Religion," (1 Dec. 1986) R006.

[71] Foreign Broadcast Information Service, "Gorbachev Meets Moscow Patriarch Aleksey II," (28 June 1991) 032.

[72] Ibid., 23-24.

[73] Ibid., 25-29.

[74] Ibid., 29-31.

[75] Kent Hill, *The Puzzle of the Soviet Church* (Portland, Ore.: Mutnomah Press, 1989), 321.

[76] Foreign Broadcast Information Service, "Gorbachev Talk With Church Leaders Lauded," (23 May 1988): 064.

[77] Foreign Broadcast Information Service, "Vatican Secretary of State Arrives in Moscow," (13 June 1988): 046.

[78] Foreign Broadcast Information Service, "Dalai Lama Praises Gorbachev; Hopes For Meeting," (22 July 1991): 029.

[79] Foreign Broadcast Information Service, "Aleksey II Says Gorbachev 'Should Be Heard'," (21 August 1991): 020.

[80] Richard Ostling, "Victory for a Dark Horse," *Time* vol. 135, no 25 (18 June 1990): 71.

[81] Foreign Broadcast Information Service, "Yeltsin Grants Patriarchate Use of Churches", (26 November 1991): 056.

[82] Foreign Broadcast Information Service, "Yeltsin Appeals to Heads of Churches, Believers," (6 December 1991): 059-60.

[83] Mikhail Sergeev, "Religious Nationalism in Russia: A Postmodern identity?", *Religion in Eastern Europe* vol. XIV, no. 2 (1994): 33-35.

www.ingramcontent.com/pod-product-compliance
Lightning Source LLC
Chambersburg PA
CBHW022113280326
41933CB00007B/376

9 7 8 0 9 8 3 3 2 1 1 3 2